First published in 2003
Published by Photoforum and Photoworks

Photoforum
c/o School of Historical and Critical Studies,
University of Brighton,
10/11 Pavilion Parade,
Brighton, BN2 1RA

Photoworks,
Kent Institute of Art and Design,
Oakwood Park,
Maidstone,
Kent, ME16 8AG
Tel: 01622-621134
Fax: 01622-62135
email: photo.works@virgin.net

Distributed by Cornerhouse Publications
70 Oxford Street,
Manchester, M1 5NH
Tel: 0161-200-1503
Fax: 0161-200-1504
email: publications@cornerhouse.org

British Library Cataloguing-in-Publication Data.
A catalogue record for this book is available from the British Library.
ISBN 1-903796-08-3

Edited by David Green
Design by LOUP
Printed by Dexter Graphics Ltd

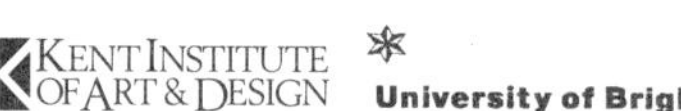

Edited by David Green

photoWORKS | **photoforum**

Contents

Acknowledgements

The majority of the essays in this volume originated in talks presented at the conference entitled *Photography, Philosophy, Technology* held in April 2002. That conference was the first to be organised by Photoforum, a collaboration between the University of Brighton, Kent Institute of Art and Design and the Surrey Institute of Art and Design University College, which was established with the principal aim of promoting critical debate concerning contemporary photography, in particular where this relates to its role in fine art practices. Other conferences and events are also planned for the future and we hope, as is the case here, to be able to reach a wider audience through the publication of their proceedings. As regards this and further publications we are extremely pleased to be working closely with Photoworks, the independent visual arts organisation that promotes photography in the South East of England.

We would like to thank, firstly and foremost, the University of Brighton, Kent Institute of Art and Design and the Surrey Institute of Art and Design University College, for their support of Photoforum. Particular thanks must be given to Dr. Paddy Maguire of the School of Historical and Critical Studies at the University of Brighton for his encouragement of Photoforum from its inception. The original conference, and therefore indirectly this volume of essays, would not have been possible without the financial support of South East Arts and the British Academy and we extend our thanks to them. Finally and most of all, of course, we have to acknowledge the goodwill and commitment of Geoff Batchen, Pavel Büchler, Steve Edwards, Laura Mulvey, Peter Osborne, Olivier Richon, Richard Shiff, whose contributions to the conference *Photography, Technology Philosophy* made that such a stimulating and enjoyable event and for their efforts in turning the papers they delivered into the essays that appear here.

Foreword

The question posed by the title of this collection of essays 'Where is the
Photograph?' emerged as the central concern in a conference entitled
Photography, Philosophy, Technology organised by Photoforum in 2002.
The drive behind this conference had been to provide a platform to discuss
some of the significant changes that had taken place in the domain of
photographic theory over the past decade. It seemed to us that during this
period the ways in which we approached and thought about the medium
of photography had undergone some important changes but that these had
rarely been fully acknowledged. If we have been, at some level, responsive
to the subtle movements in intellectual fashion, perhaps we have not been
nearly reflective enough about what the full significance of those changing
perspectives on the nature of photography might be.

The relationships between photographic practices and the theoretical and
critical modes of analysis that take photography as their object, have always
been complex and dynamic. On the one hand, photography theory has always
been susceptible to, and parasitic upon, the field of contemporary photographic
practices: as the concerns of artists and photographers have changed, so
photographic theorists have struggled to adapt to the challenges that those
practices pose for their understanding of the medium. On the other hand, it is
also the case that the photographic practices have in their turn been informed,
and sometimes guided by, ideas – often stemming from a wide range of
intellectual disciplines – which may sometimes involve radically rethinking
what photography is.

In the later 1970s and 1980s the interrelationships between theory and
practice played itself out primarily through the work of artists who sought to
re-evaluate the position of photography within the image-culture at large and
in terms of art's role viz-a-viz the mass media. These practices were closely
intertwined with a wealth of theoretical analysis, strongly influenced by post-
structuralism, psychoanalysis, feminism and post-Althusserian Marxism.
As such the analysis of photography and photographic practices took place
therefore within a discursive space that was dominated by social and political
issues. A key component in this particular intellectual formation was that the

photographic image was encountered through semiotics; that is, as a 'text' to be decoded, analysed, manipulated, and re-assembled. Photography was placed firmly within the realm of the socio-cultural and it was those disciplines that engaged in forms of analysis appropriate to this perspective that provided the context for its theorisation, one that was, more often than not, construed in terms of 'the politics of representation'.

Whilst the kinds of theoretical and critical frameworks that came to the fore in the 1980s may still be valuable, they seem to us less suitable to the questions raised by the kinds of photographic practice that have emerged in the last decade. During the 1990s photography became a ubiquitous presence in spaces of the gallery and museum but in ways in which its identity was radically reconfigured. Through its incorporation into a wide range of fine art practices, photography had increasingly to be thought of in terms of its intersection with, on the one hand, the traditional mediums of painting and sculpture, and, on the other hand, with the hybrid forms of installation and performance. At the same time, with the rapid development of evermore sophisticated electronic and digital technologies, the limits of the photographic itself have expanded. The most obvious consequence of this has been that it is now extremely difficult to say precisely where and how we are to define the boundaries that separate photography from film or video, or, indeed, any of the other forms of iconic, graphic or textual material that it is now possible to assemble and display on the computer screen. Certainly we can no longer automatically assume that the printed photographic still-image is the archetypal form of the photograph, but only one of many possible realisations of a set of technological apparatuses and practices configured around the production of the visual field. Photography, therefore, no longer has (if it ever did have) any ontological stability.

As contemporary fine art practices have become an increasingly significant arena within which concepts of the photographic have been explored, so the theoretical concerns associated with photography have changed. Contemporary artists have posed the question of our encounter with the photographic, of how we can make sense of it and read it in the first place. They have forced us to reflect upon the very strangeness of these forms of representation and of their fundamental elusiveness in the face of our search for meaning. They have drawn our attention to the ambiguity and potential undecidability of the photographic sign, its resistance to meaning, its relationship to time and history, and its indexicality. They have positioned photographs in the spaces of the gallery in ways that challenge our physical and imaginative relationship to the image. In response to these practices the questions that we ask of photography have moved away from the semiotic forms of cultural analysis and into the domains of aesthetics and phenomenology. These fundamental shifts in the theoretical and critical terrain have forced us to abandon our preconceptions about what a photograph might be or mean and to ask the more fundamental question of where, in this complex space of technology, bodies and representational practices, something called the photograph might be; what it might mean for us to identify it and try to relate it to the reality beyond; and what impact it might have upon us as subjects in a technological world.

The essays in this volume all, in their very different ways, respond to these questions. The photograph, for each of these writers, is ultimately a puzzle, something elusive and difficult to pin down. But for each of them that puzzle represents an opportunity to engage with a wider set of issues about how we encounter meaning in the modern world.

Joanna Lowry
David Green
David Campany

'fearful ghost of former bloom': What Photography Is
Geoffrey Batchen

Recently I came across an object in a New York junk store. It was large, about 87 by 82 by 20 centimetres, and was propped up on a top shelf, and therefore a little out of sight and in the shadows. All I could see at first was a big glass and timber frame and what seemed like a bunch of floral decorations in a wreath-like arrangement. Indeed, it took a moment before I noticed that this thing was actually a photographic object and therefore at least potentially within the range of my professional interests. I quickly moved aside various stuffed animals that were in the way and climbed up onto a chair to have a closer look.

What I saw there, in its centre, was an albumen photograph of a young woman, a little faded and stained around the edges but otherwise distinct. (Figure 1) She stares over my shoulder, eternally lost in her own thoughts and protected by a somewhat vacant and ethereal smile. Under this rather formulaic studio portrait I read the words "At Rest", impressed into a sheet of copper and pinned to the board behind. At each of its two top edges are rosettes, woven out of human hair (probably hers). Around all of this rests an extravagant wreath of flowers made from wax, with similarly waxen butterflies flitting decoratively amongst the petals. Some of the flowers have melted away or simply crumpled a little, adding their ruinous state of being to the sense of sadness that suffuses the whole scene. Based on the style of the object, and the type of photograph, I presume it to have been made in the later nineteenth century.

At first glance, looking back from the perspective of the present, this object appears to have been a professionally made, commercial product. However, it has to be remembered that mourning and remembering were once both pursuits considered the province of women. Until the advent of a professional 'death industry' in the late nineteenth century, women were expected to prepare the body of the deceased for burial and to lead the family in its often-elaborate grieving rituals.[1] And this included making various kinds of memorials and keepsakes dedicated to the departed. As Colleen McDannell has demonstrated, these objects often involved the sense of touch; gloves, rings, and hair art figure prominently amongst those tokens typically exchanged in memory of

1 For elements of this history, see John Morley, *Death, Heaven and the Victorians*, University of Pittsburgh Press, London, 1971; Pat Jalland, *Death in the Victorian Family*, Oxford University Press, 1996; and Gary Laderman, *The Sacred Remains: American Attitudes Toward Death, 1799-1883*, Yale University Press, New Haven & London, 1996. For a photographic history of this death industry, see Dan Meinwald, *Memento Mori: Death in 19th Century Photography*, California Museum of Photography Bulletin, 1990, and Jay Ruby, *Secure the Shadow: Death and Photography in America*, MIT Press, Cambridge, Mass., 1995.

2 Colleen McDannell, *Material Christianity: Religion and Popular Culture in America*, Yale University Press, New Haven & London, 1995.

3 Authors unknown, *Elegant Arts for Ladies*, Ward and Lock, London, 1856, p.184. Interestingly, this book also devotes a whole chapter to 'Weaving or Plaiting Hair Ornaments' including subsections on 'Plaits for Rings, Lockets, and Brooches' and on 'Mourning Devices.' It also comes with three pages of advertisements for such things as 'Barnard's Photographic Watercolours' and 'Barnard's Photographic Powder-Colours.' This same Jabez Barnard also offered books for sale titled *Wax Flowers: The Art of Modelling by Mrs Skill*, and *Wax Flowers and Fruit: The Art of Modelling by G.W. Francis*.

4 From T.B. Thorpe, 'Bessie Black, or, The Undertaker's Courtship,' *Appleton's Journal: a magazine of general literature*, New York, August 7, 1869, p.583.

the deceased.[2] On the evidence of stories and instructions published in a number of nineteenth-century English and American books and magazines with a primarily female readership, the making of wax flowers was of a similar order, one of those accomplishments middle-class women were expected to master and practice in the home. *Elegant Arts for Ladies,* published in 1856, devotes a whole chapter, for example, to the making of 'Waxen Flowers and Fruit', and includes forty-six illustrations detailing how it should be done. It also offers the following rationale: 'the practice of the art of modelling fruits and flowers in wax directs the mind to study what is beautiful and wonderful; and hence to feel, after all, how utterly beyond imitation in detail are the marvellous handiworks of the Creator!'[3] What we're looking at here, in other words, is the product of a gendered, domestic and very probably amateur craft, much like embroidery and quilting.

Stories published in nineteenth-century magazines also give us a glimpse, albeit a fictional one, into the emotions such practices both demonstrated and induced. The following is taken from a story titled '*Bessie Black, or, The Undertaker's Courtship*', published in *Appleton's Journal: a magazine of general literature* in 1869:

> *She had learned, among other simple accomplishments, in her younger days, to make wax flowers, and, in the success of her manipulations, she conceived the idea of applying her knowledge to the preservation and embalmment of funeral wreaths. Bessie was proud of them, and Mr.Hollowshell and the aristocratic coroner pronounced them 'handsomer than the real things', and the undertaker made two frames of pine-wood, and painted them to look like ebony, inclosing French plate-glass, cut from the remnants of a large pane, that had formerly made up one of the sides of his best hearse. And these mummified flowers were hung up in a conspicuous place in the undertaker's shop. They were horribly attractive and fascinating, as a rattlesnake is fascinating. It seemed as if these charming heaven-favored gifts of bounteous Nature had been frozen by a sudden breeze of wind from the wing of Death, which had left them shrivelled, shrunken, ghastly corpses of what were once flowers – their heaven-scented fragrance departed, and now smelling only of the earth from which they were born.[4]*

What is notable here is the emphasis on fragrance and a breeze; both sensorial metaphors for a spiritual ascension of the soul to heaven. The wax flowers in this wreath provide a virtual version of this same message, and it is repeated again in the wax butterflies, those signs of metamorphosis, springtime (and therefore new life), and resurrection. And as the fictional Bessie Black suggests, the replacement of real flowers with wax ones recalls the processes of embalming but it also links heaven and earth, and life to death.

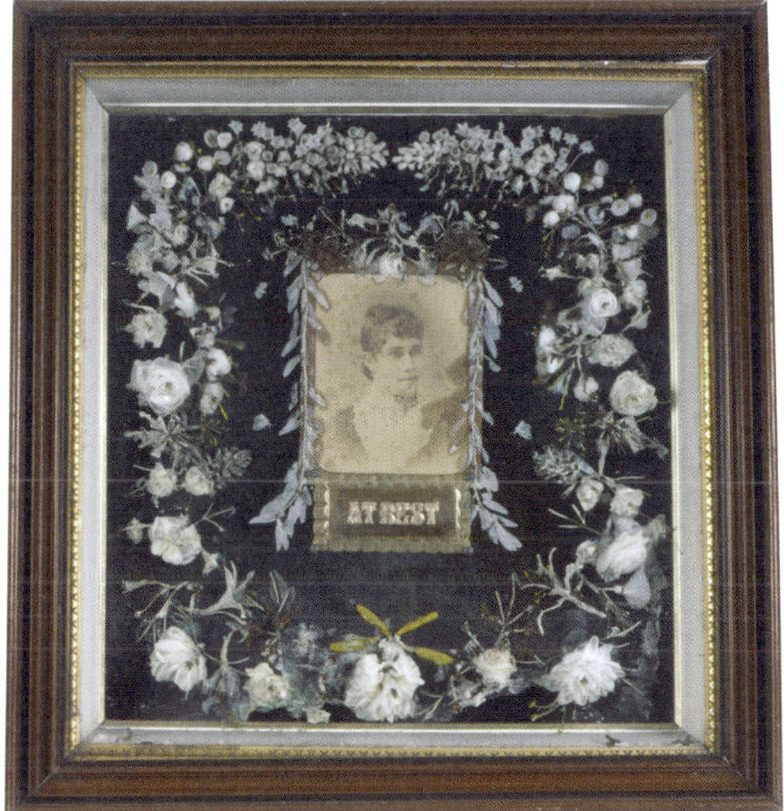

Figure 1. Makers unknown (American), *Portrait of a young woman with wax flower wreath*, c.1890.

We find a similarly morbid reading of these kinds of wreaths in a later essay titled *'The Funeral Wreath, or, The Ghost's Photograph'* written by Bessie O'Byrne and published in *Catholic World* in 1900. In this attempt at a horror-story, a group of women find themselves living alone in a newly rented house. On their first night they find an aged and dusty funeral wreath of dried flowers in a cupboard, from which drops an equally aged photograph of an obviously sick man, an apparition of whom later returns to haunt them. One of the girls speaks of the crumbling flowers themselves as the 'fearful ghost of former bloom' and asks herself 'why do people want to torture themselves by preserving such private and individual racks whereon to stretch their own sensibilities?'[5]

5 Bessie O'Byrne, 'The Funeral Wreath, or, The Ghost's Photograph', *Catholic World*, 72: 428, November 1900, pp.176-194.

It's a good question. But before we investigate it a little further, we should consider the object I found in the New York junk shop a little more closely. To begin, we would have to concede that this is a challenging kind of object on any number of levels. For a start, it doesn't fit easily into the art history of photography that we still usually encounter in books and museums devoted to the medium. And it's these historical discourses that traditionally have decided what photography is and isn't, defining the boundaries of the medium, at least for academics and the market place. Up until now, neither photography museums nor survey histories of photography have cared to include hybrid objects like this within those boundaries.[6] Can it, therefore, even be called 'photography'?

True, it does have a photograph, and this is centrally placed in the overall scheme of things, but the main visual impact of the piece comes from its substantial frame and its wax wreath. Neither the photographer nor the subject, nor the maker of the wreath or frame, are named, so no colourful biographical details or aesthetic intentions are available to animate its story. It remains, then, an obdurately anonymous object, comprised of a number of different materials, with some added text in case we didn't already get the meaning of the iconography, and taking up the sort of space we normally concede to 'sculpture'.

And then there is its subject matter. Death is a difficult-enough subject to represent at the best of times, but here it is replete with fully-fledged, Victorian, bourgeois sentiment, and with none of the self-conscious irony that is so fashionable today.[7] This points to one of the other problems this object poses. I've been brought up to believe that the function of good art history (that's my university affiliation and academic training) is to focus on avant-garde practice, because the artistic avant-garde supposedly represents a space of resistance to the blandishments of globalized capital. Good historical criticism should privilege this space, thereby offering an alternative model of practice (both artistic and social/political) to that continually propagated by and embodied in the products of a normative capitalist culture. But this object appears to be neither avant-garde nor obviously politically charged.

There are lots of problems to be addressed here, and many of them have to do with issues important to photography, issues like identity and history, issues that reflect on the very being of photography, on the question of 'what photography is'.

Perhaps the first thing to recognise is that, although "At Rest" is a necessarily unique object, it is also a typical product of the later nineteenth century. We could compare it, for example, to another version of the same kind of thing, only even more elaborate in its spectacularisation of grief and remembrance. This one was found in a junk store in Albuquerque, New Mexico. It's large

6 For more on this exclusion, see Geoffrey Batchen, 'Vernacular Photographies,' *Each Wild Idea: Writing, Photography, History,* MIT Press, Cambridge, Mass., 2001, pp. 56-80, 199-204.

7 Roland Barthes, *Camera Lucida: Reflections on Photography,* Hill and Wang, New York, 1980.

again, about 85 by 77 by 21 centimetres, and its deep box frame has even more
stuff in it than my first example. (Figure 2) The central place is once again given
to a photograph, an albumen cabinet card, this time of a young man photographed in Minnesota (by P.E. Lynne of Crookston), incorporating a stylised
scroll motif. Above him are two white doves (taxidermy being a popular home
craft for boys in this period). These doves have apparently been caught exactly
in mid-flight, one the mirror image of the other, both a little glassy-eyed but
still faithfully clutching ears of wheat in their beaks. Beneath them can be read
the now-familiar words "At Rest," here inscribed in brown fabric disguised to
look like some sort of organic material. There are also some words clustered
around the photograph, "There Rest He In Sweet Heaven" written in purple
pipe cleaners. The inside edge of the gilt box frame is filled with green fabric
leaves and waxed-paper rosettes. I suspect this object was made a little later
than its counterpart, perhaps around 1910, but incorporating a cabinet card
made in a previous decade.

Memory is here given a physical manifestation. Or perhaps it would
be more accurate to say that this object is primarily dedicated to a fear of
forgetting. Why else would it so anxiously reiterate the same basic message
over and over again? Mingling Christian iconography (the dove of peace
and resurrection, sign of the Holy Ghost) with a secular, mechanical image
(a photograph of the deceased), it speaks of death and mourning but also of
a renewal of life. It seeks to remember this man, not as someone now dead,
but as someone who was once alive, young and vital, with a future before him.
And in this object he still has.

Faced with such an ensemble, one can't avoid recalling Barthes' famous
incantation over the image of another young man with death before him: 'I
read at the same time: *This will be* and *this has been*; I observe with horror an
anterior future of which death is the stake... I shudder *over a catastrophe which
has already occurred.*'[8] Barthes would seem to share this morbid fascination
with those nineteenth-century magazine writers from whom I have already
quoted. But perhaps they all need to look again.

Barthes starts from the photograph, from what once was life, and then
looks forward, like a seer, to a future death, a death that, in the case of the
Gardner photograph he is discussing, has by then already occurred. But here,
with this framed object, we must start with the fact of this man's death, a fact
signified by all the insistent iconographic paraphernalia arrayed around him,
and then we look back (literally, into the depths of the object, as well as back
through time) to a moment when he was still alive. It is the exact reverse of
Barthes' temporal narrative, and thus also allows for a different outcome, for
a celebration rather than a shuddering. By shifting the pall of death from the

8 ibid, 96.

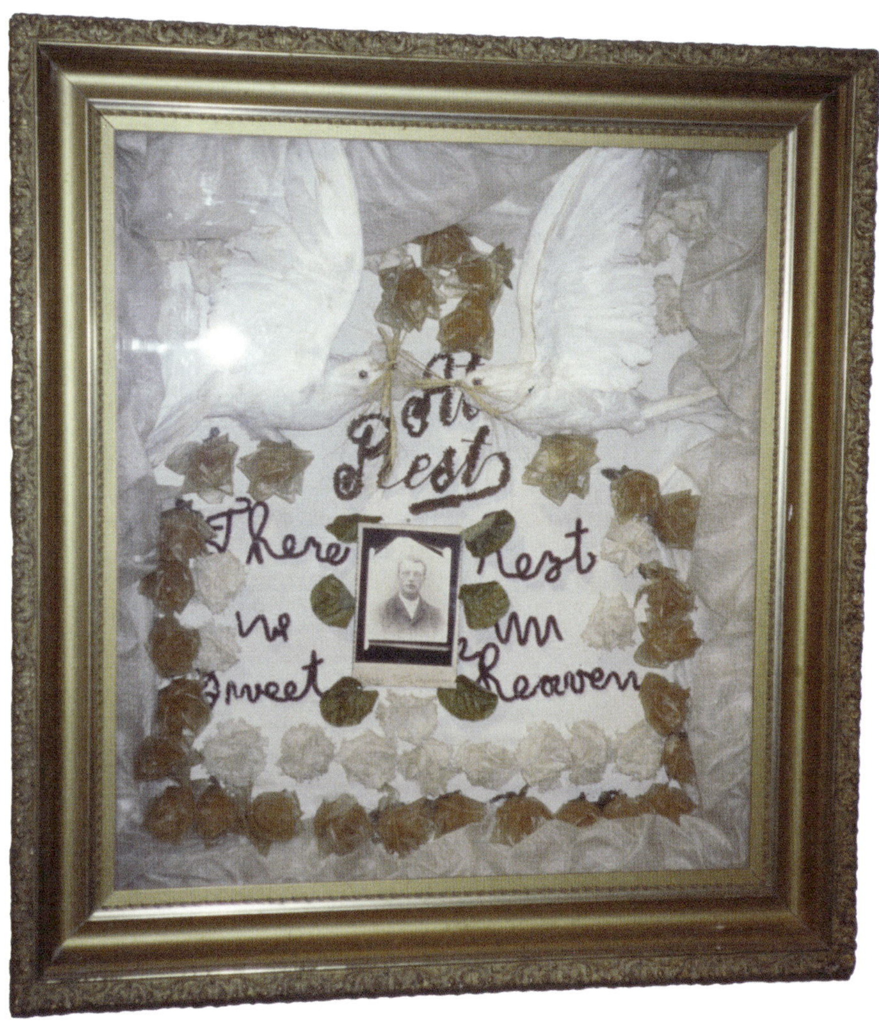

Figure 2. Makers unknown (American) *Memorial to a Young Man*, c.1910.

photograph to its surrounds, this object declares that Life, rather than Death, is the 'eidos' of its photograph. The photographed subject is still a ghost of his former self, but here that ghost haunts with the comforting presence of an eternal life rather than with the morbid reminder of a perpetual death.

So this type of object speaks to a quite particular articulation of time, and thus to matters of life and death. Its elaborate hybridity enables it to reverse the usual temporal character of the photograph that it incorporates, and to contest even the quotidian wisdom of a Roland Barthes. But it speaks, as well, of a whole vernacular tradition involving photographs that has yet to be acknowledged by those discourses devoted to the medium, a tradition in which the photograph sometimes plays only a bit part, but in which 'photography' as a concept continues to occupy a central role.

I will return to this point. But first it seems important to establish the outlines of this genre and identify its basic characteristics. Only then, after tracing a history for a practice not usually regarded as being a part of photography's history, can we return to the question of 'what photography is' (or isn't).

Whilst from my first two examples it might be assumed that this is a peculiarly American practice, this is not the case. If one visits, for example, the House der Fotografie in Burghausen, near Munich on the border of Germany and Austria, one finds that an important local tradition in the later nineteenth century was the surrounding of photographs with wreaths woven from dried flowers and human hair.

In this tradition a visual trace of the body of the deceased is encircled, embraced, accentuated, by portions of that same body. Photography's much-vaunted truth to presence is joined by the actual presence of a piece of the body being signified. Strange though it may seem to us today, the addition of human hair to memorial objects was in fact a common practice by the early decades of the nineteenth century. As Thomas Laqueur notes, hair began to enjoy a new prominence as the raw material of memory. 'It became the corporeal auto-icon par excellence, the favoured synecdoche – the real standing for the symbolic – perhaps not eternally incorruptible but long lasting enough, a bit of a person that lives eerily on as a souvenir.'[9]

Hair, intimate and yet easily detached, is of course a convenient and pliable stand-in for the whole body of the missing, memorialised subject. In the nineteenth century, women in particular were encouraged to use hair in their domestic handicrafts, beginning with horse hair and then, as their skills improved, working with the finer human hair, either bought for the purpose or gathered from friends or even from their own heads. Braiding tables were available to facilitate the production of complex patterns and braids, and books were published with instructions on the various methods and styles available.[10]

9 Thomas Laqueur, 'Clio Looks at Corporal Politics', *Corporal Politics*, exhibition catalogue, MIT List Visual Arts Center, Cambridge, Mass., 1992, pp.16-17.

10 By 1862, advertisements for 'artists in hair' were appearing in such journals as the *Illustrated London News*. In 1855 a full-length, life-size portrait of Queen Victoria, composed only of hair, had been exhibited at the Paris Exhibition. See Deirdre O'Day, *Victorian Jewellery*, Charles Letts Books, London, 1982, p.36. See also Mary Trasko, *Daring Do's: A History of Extraordinary Hair*, Flammarion, Paris-New York, 1994 and Mark Campbell, *Self-Instructor in the Art of Hair Work: Hair Braiding and Jewelry of Sentiment, with a Catalog of Hair Jewelry* (1875 edition), Jules and Kaethe Kliot eds. Lacis Publications, Berkeley, Cal., 1994.

11 See Marcia Pointon, 'These Fragments I have Shored against my Ruins', in Kristen Lippincott, ed., *The Story of Time*, Merrell Holberton & National Maritime Museum, London, 1999, pp.198-201, 293.

12 This is a paraphrase of the title of an oil painting in the collections of the Tate Gallery, London: H.A. Bowler's *The Doubt: 'Can these Dry Bones Live?* c.1856.

13 Régis Durand, 'How to See (Photographically)', in Patrice Petro ed., *Fugitive Images: From Photography to Video*, Indiana University Press, Bloomington, 1995), p. 146. On this question of fetishism, see also Marcia Pointon, 'Materializing Mourning: Hair, Jewellery and the Body,' in Marius Kwint, Christopher Breward and Jeremy Aynsley, eds., *Material Memories*, Berg, Oxford, 1999), pp. 39-57.

14 See Geoffrey Batchen, 'A Perfect Likeness,' in Helen Ennis ed., *Mirror with a Memory: Photographic Portraiture in Australia*, National Portrait Gallery, Canberra, 2000, pp. 27-36.

Such activities had a theological as well as an aesthetic significance. Speaking of the addition of hair to jewellery in this same period, Marcia Pointon reports that 'the use of hair...seems to be a peculiarly Christian practice' stemming from a particular reading of the book of Revelations, such that a lock of hair becomes a sign of a possible reunion with the deceased in the afterlife.[11] So once again we find that this photo-object is attempting to transcend the brutal fact of death with the uplifting promise of eternal life. It seeks to offer an optimistic answer to the moment of theological doubt every mourner must feel at the interment of their loved one's body: 'Can These Dry Bones Live Again?'.[12]

But the addition of hair to these objects also declares that the photograph alone is not sufficient; not sufficient, that is, if this object is to function at all the levels being demanded of it. A photo of "MR" in the collection of the House der Fotografie in Burghausen is presumably thought in itself to be lacking something that the addition of a hair wreath fulfils, but, equally, the hair alone is also deemed to be not quite enough – apparently neither is as effective an act of representation without the other also being present (Figure 3). The hair sample stands in for the whole body of the absent subject, turning this ensemble into a modern fetish object. In the words of Régis Durand, as a mode of representation it 'allow[s] me to believe that what is missing is present all the same, *even though I know* it is not the case'.[13] A piece of the body is used to add a sort of sympathetic magic to the already magical processes of photography, a little insurance against separation, whether temporary or permanent. By this means, as I've already suggested, a secular object is given a potentially sacred aspect.

But the hybridity of this object also makes for a stronger portrait experience. By adding a sample of hair to the subject's photograph, the indexical presence of that subject is reiterated and reinforced. Indeed, the merger of natural material (hair) and cultural sign (wreath) is a repetition of photography's own distinctive implosion of nature and culture (an implosion embodied in the very word 'photography,' from the Greek meaning 'light-writing'). By this addition to the photograph, the 'studium' of mere resemblance (and this portrait is of the formulaic kind that offers little more than this) is transformed into the 'punctum' of the subject-as-ghost (a figure simultaneously absent and present, alive and dead). Combining visibility with touch (both real and imagined), this object might be regarded as an effort to directly link the photograph, the body of "MR" and the body of the viewer, a much more involving type of portrait experience than any single, unadulterated photograph could provide. The object's hybridity thereby helps bridge the distance between the viewer and the person viewed and between likeness and subject (between mere resemblance and that something more promised by the word 'portrait').[14]

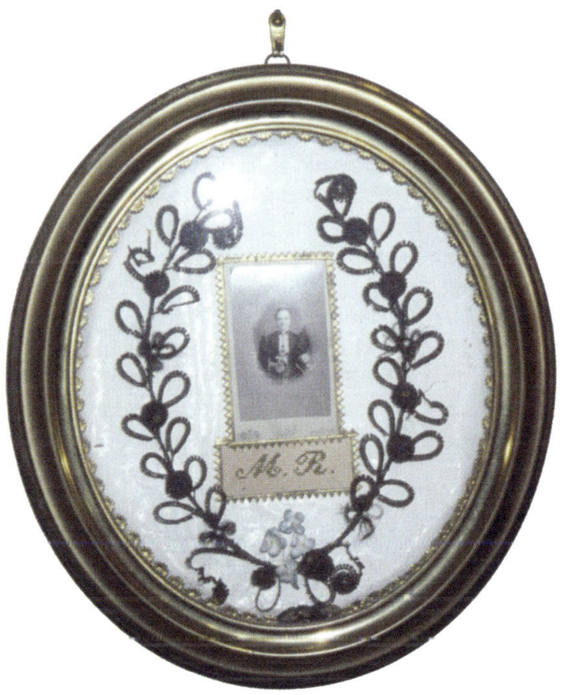

Figure 3. Maker unknown
(German), *Portrait of a woman*,
c.1890.

This bridging is important because, of course, although we are here mourning the death of another, we are also meditating on mortality in general, on our own imminent passing and potential loss of self.

This photograph comes with a text, the words "MR" embroidered as the caption to a cabinet card of the young woman concerned. The fact that only this woman's initials are inscribed within the object suggests that it was meant for private consumption, for the contemplation of just those who already knew both her full name and her full self. Other clues reinforce this impression. Her portrait has been vignetted to delete the man standing beside her; his strangely dismembered arm is all that remains of him, entwined lovingly with her own. Her other, free hand clutches a small bouquet of flowers, a symbolic remnant of which now rests in the cradle of the hair wreath. The generic pose and iconography strongly suggests that this photograph was originally taken as a wedding portrait of the once-happy couple. Could it be that, on MR's untimely death, her husband has returned to the negative and had himself partially deleted from the original image, leaving her as the only entirely visible subject? This photograph now speaks of her, of how she once looked, but also of the emotional violence of their enforced separation. Equally, photography is revealed as a practice of reproduction, even while every effort has been made here to ensure this particular reproduction is a unique and individual one.

So what are we to make of all these combinations of photograph and wreath? The very ubiquity of this combination calls for a brief history of the wreath as a visual form. The wearing of garlands made from flowers or leaves goes back to the time of the ancient Greeks; a wreath of laurel leaves was worn, for example, by victors at the Olympics from 776 BC. The Romans used garlands of evergreens to celebrate the winter solstice in honour of their god Saturn. This pagan symbolism gradually became absorbed into Christian tradition, with funeral garlands first recorded in connection with the burial of virgins, and especially of virgin martyrs, to symbolize their victory over death. Wreaths were once hung above graves or in churches, but even when placed flat on a wall, as in most of these cases, they still contiguously reference the head of the deceased and the hand of the maker, creating a kind of bond between them.[15]

The circular shape of these wreaths is itself a symbol of eternity, while the flowers and leaves that comprise them represent life and regrowth; thus, as a complete sign, the funeral wreath promises resurrection and eternal life. Most flowers and plants had distinct and recognisable meanings in Victorian times, such that cypress and willow signified mourning, and laurel equalled victory over death.[16] Flowering plants also give off a smell, perhaps helpful in covering that of the decaying corpse but also adding another memorial sense to one's sight (as well as wafting heavenwards). In almost all the cases mentioned here, however, the wreaths are made out of materials other than real flowers, providing only an imagined smell but at least allowing a permanency of image (in the presence of these wreaths, it's always springtime). In this sense, the floral wreath is like the photograph it encircles, recalling and imitating the look of a subject now physically absent; in both cases they are truly a 'fearful ghost of former bloom'.

But objects like these also offer a sceptical commentary on the capacity of photography to provide a suitable memory experience. We usually imagine photographs and memories to be synonymous. The American writer Oliver Wendell Holmes called photography 'the mirror with a memory' as early as 1859, and the Eastman Kodak company has extensively promoted this notion ever since: '[Kodak] enables the fortunate possessor to go back by the light of his own fireside to scenes which would otherwise fade from memory and be lost'.[17] And so we have taken our photographs, voraciously and anxiously, as if to fail to do so would be to let our precious memories fade away into the mists of time and amnesia.

15 Flowers and wreaths have not only been of significance for Europeans. See Bobbi Salinas, *Indo-Hispanic Folk Art Traditions II: The Day of the Dead and other year-round activities*, Pinata, Fort Worth, Texas, 1988.

16 See Diana Cooper and Norman Battershill, *Victorian Sentimental Jewellery*, A.S. Barnes & Co., South Brunswick & New York, 1973, pp. 72-82.

17 Oliver Wendell Holmes, 'The Stereoscope and the Stereograph,' *The Atlantic Monthly*, 3, June 1859, pp. 728-48. On Kodak's attempts to ally its photography with memory, see James E. Paster, 'Advertising Immortality by Kodak,' *History of Photography*, 16: 2, Summer 1992, pp. 135-140, and Nancy Martha West, *Kodak and the Lens of Nostalgia*, University Press of Virginia, Charlottesville, 2000.

The irony in all this is that some of photography's most insightful critics have argued that in fact photography and memory do not mix, that one even precludes the other. Barthes, for example, claimed that 'not only is the Photograph never, in essence, a memory...but it actually blocks memory, quickly becomes a counter-memory'.[18] Following Proust's lead in *Remembrance of Things Past*, Barthes bases his claim on the presumed capacity of the photograph to replace the immediate, physically embracing experience of involuntary memory (the sort of emotional responses most often induced, before conscious thought, by smells and sounds) with frozen illustrations set in the past; photography replaces the unpredictable thrill of memory with the dull certainties of history.[19]

However in the examples I've been discussing here, the photograph's capacity to erase memory has been countered by its transformation into an overtly touched and/or touchable object-form. In the process, the subject of each photograph has been similarly transformed, from something merely seen into someone really felt, from just an image set in the past into an exchange you are emotionally touched by right now in the present. Turned into fetish objects devoted to the cult of remembrance, hybrid photographs such as this ask us to give up a little something of ourselves if they are to function satisfactorily. They demand the projection onto their constituent stuff of our own bodies, but also of our personal recollections, hopes and fears (about the passing of time, about death, about being remembered only as history, and – most terrible of all – about being forgotten altogether).

All this enhances the photograph's capacity to conjure memory, and this at a time when, according to Richard Terdiman, memory itself is in a state of crisis.[20] Of course, memory is always in crisis, always in fearful struggle with its other, with the encroachment of amnesia.[21] We've already seen that many of these hybrid photo-objects assume memories to be fragile, impossible to pin down, mutable, able to be experienced only in an interactive and often intensely personal moment of perception. But Terdiman regards the nineteenth century as a period in which this perpetual memory crisis takes on a more social and systematic character, driven by the often-bewildering changes wrought by political revolution and industrial modernity. He argues that Europeans of this period 'experienced the insecurity of their culture's involvement with its past', a type of memory crisis in which 'the very coherence of time and of subjectivity seemed disarticulated'. He points to, among other nineteenth-century texts, the commentary in Karl Marx's *Capital* on commodity fetishism, suggesting that, 'because commodities suppress the memory of their own process'; 'essentially, "reification" is a memory disturbance: *the enigma of the commodity is a memory disorder*'.[22] Indeed, memory is one of

18 Barthes, *Camera Lucida*, p. 91.

19 See Roland Barthes, 'From Taste to Ecstasy' (1980) and 'On Photography' (1980), in *The Grain of the Voice: Interviews 1962-1980*, trans. Linda Coverdale, University of California Press, Berkeley, 1985, pp.351-360.

20 Richard Terdiman, *Present Past: Modernity and the Memory Crisis*, Cornell University Press, Ithaca, NY, 1993.

21 Marita Sturken, *Tangled Memories: The Vietnam War, The AIDS Epidemic, and the Politics of Remembering*, University of California Press, Berkeley, 1997, p.7, p.17.

22 Terdiman, op. cit., pp. 3-4, 12.

those abstractions increasingly reified in the nineteenth century, turned into lucrative commercial objects of exchange such as keepsakes and souvenirs. One might regard the invention and proliferation of photography as both a response to this memory crisis but also as its embodiment and reproduction. The photograph remembers a loved one's appearance, but it is a memory 'hollowed out,' disconnected from the social realities of its own production, and also from us, who are doing the remembering. In giving us no more than a likeness of the absent person, the photograph also distances us from what Barthes called 'the air,' or being, of this person, from 'a subject – in Mallarmé's terms – "as *into* itself eternity transforms it"'.[23]

23 Barthes, *Camera Lucida*, pp.102-103.

Might we regard these various vernacular practices – in which the photograph is touched, worked on, added to, transformed into a personalised, handmade object and a multi-sensory experience – as an attempted complication of, or even counter to, this same memory crisis? They all enact a practice that breaches the virtual walls of the photographic image, forcing us to simultaneously project our mind's eye back and forth, into and out of, the photograph they incorporate. They punctuate the 'chafed reality' of time, for Barthes the *noeme* or essence of the photographic experience, with the more immediate and tangible realities of physical space. They collapse looking into touching, and history into memory, and, by making their photographs relatively minor, if never incidental, elements of a larger ensemble, they refuse to privilege a pure photography over other types of representational experience.

By this means they also offer a kind of commentary on photography itself as a representational system. Placed in a substantial wooden frame and surrounded by other materials, the photograph is turned into a physical thing, a thing whose perception requires our hands as well as our eyes. No longer can the photograph pose as if simply transparent to the world it signifies. Framed in tangible materials, and then framed again by the real and/or imagined touch of a loved one's hand, the photograph in these objects cannot help becoming a sign of itself as well as of its referent. These photographs are now themselves objects, and this calls attention to that aspect of photographs usually repressed in our consciousness of them, their physical presence as things. And once revealed as a thing among other things, and as a sign among signs, photography's very process of formation, its indexical relationship to a world outside of itself, is called into question-or at least posed *as* a question.

As Jacques Derrida recognizes in his own discussion of indexicality, 'the thing itself is a sign…from the moment there is meaning there are nothing but signs'.[24] And this declaration could surely now be extended to encompass all the identities incorporated in these vernacular objects (nature and culture, the human body and its ghosts, remembering and forgetting, the literal and

24 Jacques Derrida, *Of Grammatology*, trans. Gayatri Spivak, University of Chicago Press, Chicago, 1976, pp. 48-50.

the abstract, the subject and the viewer); in every case, real and representation
are made to continually signal and (de)generate the other. In short, these
hybrid photo-objects are a physical manifestation of, in Derrida's words, 'the
impossibility for an identity to be closed in on itself, on the inside of its proper
interiority, or on its coincidence with itself'.[25]

I suggested earlier that the identity of photography has in many ways been
delimited by the historical discourses we have constructed around it. But, in
keeping with the complication described above, we might equally observe that,
whether consciously or unconsciously, many histories of the medium have
come to mimic their author's particular view of 'what photography is.' For
example, Beaumont Newhall's various editions of *The History of Photography*,
published between 1937 and 1982, progressively conform more and more
closely to a conventional modernist understanding of photography's identity.[26]

One crucial influence on Newhall's notion of photography was his friend
Ansel Adams, a member of the f-64 group of photographers, and, like them,
someone who believed 'that the greatest aesthetic beauty, the fullest power of
expression, the real worth of the medium lies in its pure form'.[27] Opposed to
Pictorialism in favour of a hermetic, formalist tradition established by Alfred
Stieglitz and Edward Weston, the f-64 group advocated a type of photography
in which there was no manipulation, cropping, or retouching of the
photographic print; only so-called 'straight photography' was thought to have
'real worth'. Newhall's history is organised to match this ideal: its clear,
accessible and objective-sounding prose follows a linear chronology of
technical and aesthetic innovations, mostly achieved by European or
American men.

This privileging of a modernist formalism, in which the definition of
'what photography is' is confined to properties supposedly embodied inside
the photograph's edges, was projected backwards onto photography's history.
This meant, for example, that when Newhall came to reproduce daguerreotypes
and tintypes, only the image is shown; no sign of the original matt or casing is
illustrated. Equally, photographic practices that involved adulterating the pure
photograph with other materials are ignored altogether. Given these organising
principles, it comes as no surprise to find that the kinds of objects I have been
discussing – hybrid, conventional, generic, largely amateur, and mostly made
by anonymous women – do not make an appearance in the Newhall pantheon.

One might expect a more sophisticated engagement with historical
method in the most recent of photography's survey texts, Michel Frizot's
massive anthology titled *A New History of Photography*. And indeed its
introduction by Frizot recognizes Newhall's art historical model, 'with its
almost biological evolutionary periods of genesis, vocation, maturity, and

25 Jacques Derrida, *Positions*,
trans. Alan Bass, University
of Chicago Press, Chicago,
1981, p. 94. I make a parallel
argument to the one in this
essay in my 'Ere the Substance
Fade: Photography and Hair
Jewellery,' in Elizabeth Edwards
and Janice Hart eds.,
Photographs, Objects, Histories,
Routledge, London
(forthcoming).

26 Beaumont Newhall,
The History of Photography,
Museum of Modern Art, New
York, 1982. For the background
to the writing of the first, 1937,
edition, see Allison Bertrand,
'Beaumont Newhall's
"Photography 1839-1937":
Making History,' *History of
Photography*, 21: 2, Summer,
1997, pp. 137-146.

27 John Paul Edwards,
'Camera Craft', March 1935,
in Beaumont Newhall ed.,
Photography: Essays & Images,
Museum of Modern Art,
New York, 1980, p. 251.

28 Michel Frizot, ed.,
A New History of Photography,
Kônneman, 1998, p.10, p.12.

29 Meaghan Morris, as cited
in Karen Burns, *Urban Tourism,
1851-53: Sightseeing,
Representation and The Stones
of Venice*, (PhD dissertation)
The University of Melbourne,
Melbourne, 1999, p. 310.

30 Homi Bhabha, as quoted in
Ann Stephen, 'A Hybrid Site,'
Agenda: Contemporary Art,
no. 28, Summer 1992/3,
pp.19-21. 'The hybrid site is the
moment that opens up through
something that has been
disavowed, a reinscription of
that disavowal; but it is also a
moment of the displacement
of the previous antagonism,
and indeed it opens up because
that antagonism cannot be
contained within it'.

decadence', as one thing his own history has to overcome. Frizot's definition of photography is an admirably complex one, simultaneously philosophical, technical and social, leading him to propose a history organised around photographic functions, an episodic consideration of photographs as 'working objects in their own time'.[28] In practice, this history takes on the form and structure of an illustrated news magazine, with a variety of authors contributing their own stories about particular photographic practices, and each chapter sporting periodic side-bars on a related topic. Frizot's is an undoubtedly thoughtful approach to a tough problem and he deserves credit for producing the best survey text now available. And yet we once again find hybrid vernacular practices given short thrift in this volume, either scattered through the index or herded into a single chapter, the last of forty-one and therefore relegated to the margins of the book's presentation of 'what photography is.' What we don't find is a historical morphology sympathetic to the complex photographic identity embodied in the objects under consideration here.

But what would such a morphology look, or, more pertinently, read, like? How can we develop a way of dealing with these objects that emulates their own way of being, that acknowledges rather than represses their particular qualities and characteristics? What is probably already apparent is that vernacular photographic practices issue a challenge to existing histories of photography, calling not simply for inclusion in the medium's grand narratives but for the total transformation of the narrative itself.

For a start, our history would have to acknowledge that any definition of identity based on notions of purity is simply not going to be adequate to the vast range of 'photographies' that have been produced over the past two hundred years. We have already noted that the object with which I began was almost certainly produced by a woman within a context in which women were designated as the keepers of memory and mourning rituals. So we need a history that can cope with modernities other than just those avant-garde versions associated with urban, white men. I obviously agree with Meaghan Morris when she says that, 'I prefer to study...the everyday, the so-called banal, the supposedly un-or-non-experimental, asking not "why does it fall short of modernism?" but: "how do classical theories of modernism fall short of women's modernity?"'.[29] Equally, we need an approach to our object that can engage yet further differentiations within the history of this modernity. In these objects, for example, we see the juxtaposition of a mechanical, industrial process – photography – with pre-industrial hand-crafts and rituals. It's an example of what Homi Bhabha has called a 'contra-modernity', a disjunction in which the values of the centre have been peripheralised, or at least complicated to interesting, and potentially political, effect.[30]

But as far as historical method is concerned, perhaps my object's greatest provocation is the shifts of voice it demands from its interpreter. To do it justice, we surely need to speak cogently and coherently about the past and its social histories and meanings, but also be able to conjure the 'punctum' of a very real personal grief, right here in the present. And Barthes' *Camera Lucida* is, perhaps, the most pertinent model. This shifting from past to present (and back again), and from third to first person, might at least begin to register the complexity of the identity we have encountered in these objects. For, as Stuart Hall has written: 'It [identity] belongs to the future as much as to the past. It is not something which already exists, transcending place, time, history and culture. Cultural identities come from somewhere, have histories. But, like everything else that is historical, they undergo constant transformation. Far from being eternally fixed in some essentialised past, they are subject to the continuous 'play' of history, culture and power.'[31]

And so it is with photography too. 'What photography is' is not something that already exists, some essence waiting to be retrieved from the past; it is – adopting Hall's terminology – subject to a 'continuous play of history, culture and power'. It is, like the objects we have examined here, something always caught in a process of becoming. What I have tried to demonstrate is that, if it is ever to become a truly photographic discourse, our history writing must adopt this same hybrid, open-ended, politically-charged, and sometimes even contradictory process.

This essay is much the better for the various suggestions
generously offered by Catherine Whalen, and I thank her.

31 Stuart Hall, 'Cultural Identity and Diaspora,' in Jonathan Rutherford ed., *Identity: Community, Culture, Difference,* Lawrence & Wishart, New York, 1990, p. 225.

A 'pariah in the world of art': Richter in reverse gear
Steve Edwards

Arguably, some of the best recent writing on the history of photography has developed out of an investigation of the role of photography in Conceptual Art and the related practices of photo-painting associated with Gerhard Richter, Vija Celmins, Ed Ruscha and others. In this essay I want to try to relate, if not to mediate, two important theoretical perspectives that have been concerned with this body of work: on the one hand, there are those theorists concerned with Adorno's aesthetics (I have in mind Benjamin Buchloh, Peter Osborne and John Roberts), and on the other hand, there are those who read the history of photography *figurally* (the best version of which, I believe, is to be found in the writing of Richard Shiff).[1] In order to set the idea of the photo-painting as a place-holder for the utopian possibility in the face of the culture industry against a morphology of photographic figuration drawn out of Shiff's writings, I want to replay (or reverse) some of the components of the recent debate on painting and photography back through the 1860s. In particular, I am going to consider some of the ways that history adheres to the photograph's character as a sign that bears a causal relation to its model or object: that is to say its status as an indexical sign.[2]

Let me begin with a selection of fragments from the 'expanded field' of Conceptual Art. In a famous interview from 1965 Ed Ruscha claimed:

> *Above all, the photographs I use are not 'arty' in any sense of the word. I think photography is dead as a fine art; its only place is in the commercial world, for technical or information purposes. I don't mean cinema photography, but still photography, that is, limited edition, individual, hand-processed photos. Mine are simply reproductions of photos. Thus, it is not a book to house a collection of art photographs – they are technical data like industrial photography. To me, they are nothing more than snapshots.*[3]

In this fascinating paragraph the commercial, or the technical, or information, is counterposed to the 'arty', which is equated with the individual and handmade. Vernacular forms such as industrial photographs, or snapshots, are thus placed outside the domain of art. The critics caught on to the Duchampian resonance of Ruscha's 'reproductions of photos' extremely quickly. In 1963 Philip Leider compared *Twenty-Six Gasoline Stations* to

1 See Benjamin Buchloh's, 'A Note on Gerhard Richter's October 18, 1977', *October* No. 48, 1989, pp.88-109 Peter Osborne's, 'Painting Negation: Gerhard Richter's Negatives', *October*, No. 62, 1992, pp.103-113 and 'Sign and Image', *Philosophy in Cultural Studies*, Routledge, 2000, pp.20-52; John Roberts', *The Impossible Document: Photography and Conceptual Art in Britain 1966-1976*, Camerawords, 1997 and *The Art of Interruption: Realism, Photography and the Everyday*, Manchester University Press, 1998; Richard Shiff's, 'Mastercopy', *Iris*, Vol. 1, 1983, pp. 113-27, 'Making a Find: An Argument for Creativity, Not Originality', *Structuralist Review*, Vol. 2, 1984, pp.59-80, 'Representation, Copying, and the Technique of Originality', *New Literary History*, No. 15, Winter, 1984, pp.333-63, 'The Original, the Imitation, the Copy, and the Spontaneous Classic: Theory and Painting in Nineteenth-Century France', *Yale French Studies*, Vol. 66, 1984, pp.27-54, and especially 'Phototropism (Figuring the Proper)', *Studies in the History of Art*, Volume. 20, 1989, pp.161-170;

2 For the indexical sign see
Charles Sanders Pierce's classic
typology of signs: 'Logic as
Semiotic: The Theory of Signs',
Justus Buchler ed., *Philosophical
Writings of Pierce*, Dover, 1955,
pp. 98-119. I need to say, at
this point, that Shiff, in his
important essay 'Phototropism:
Figuring the Proper', marks his
distance from any idea of the
photograph as an indexical
imprint of its model, preferring
instead a dynamic opposition
between, what he calls, the
'figured' and the 'proper'. In
his account, both terms are in
fact figured, even if the proper
appears, in definite conjunctures,
to occupy the position of the
literal term. I have an argument
about this, which I cannot go in
to here: instead I'm going to
use the terms index and proper
as if they were compatible. See
Shiff, 'Phototropism: Figuring
the Proper', op. cit.

3 John Coplans, 'Concerning
"Various Small Fires":
Edward Ruscha Discusses
His Perplexing Publications.'
Artforum, Vol. 3, No. 5, 1965,
pp.25.

4 Philip Leider, 'Books
Received', *Artforum*, Vol 2,
No. 3, September, 1963, p.57.

5 Coplans, op. cit. p.25.

6 Jeff Wall, '"Marks of
Indifference": Aspects of Photo-
graphy In, Or As, Conceptual
Art', in Ann Goldstein and
Anne Rorimer, *Reconsidering the
Object of Art: 1965-1975*, MIT,
1996, p. 261.

Duchamp's *Fountain* and, in the 1965 interview already cited, John Coplans specifically asks Ruscha about his relation to the ready-made.[4] This Duchampian frame has played a prominent role in accounts of these 'perplexing publications' ever since. The point ought to be apparent, where Duchamp expressed his desire to produce works that were not 'of art', Ruscha employed the photograph as an indexical sign to escape the condition of being 'of art'. These were images that were not images: they were, Ruscha claimed, 'simply a collection of "facts"'. The book itself was, he said, 'like a collection of Readymades'.[5]

Perhaps the most systematic and ambitious account of the role of photography in art in the 1960s has been provided by Jeff Wall in his essay *'Marks of Indifference': Aspects of Photography In, Or As, Conceptual Art*. Wall's chief claim is that, since the 1920s, serious photographic practice has necessarily entailed examining the liminal zones between autonomous art and the utilitarian document – a process he describes as 'gaming with the anaesthetic' – and which reaches its climax in Conceptual Art. According to Wall:

> The anaesthetic found its emblem in the Readymade, the commodity in all its guises, forms, and traces. Working-class, lower-middle class, suburbanite, and underclass milieux were expertly scoured for the relevant utilitarian images, depictions, figurations, and objects that violated all the criteria of canonical modernist taste, style and technique.[6]

In this essay Wall provides a fascinating and productive account of the dynamic relationships between 'high' and 'low' in the photographic work of Ed Ruscha, Dan Graham, and Robert Smithson, all of whom have played an important role in other recent accounts of art's relationship to photography.[7] But perhaps the privileged site for the examination of contemporary art's relation to photography has been Gerhard Richter's paintings. Richter's photo-paintings have been seen to systematically ruin modernist ideology. Benjamin Buchloh, and others, have argued that Richter's attempt to make photographs with paint occupies a pivotal moment in the history of modern art because these works transform painting itself into a readymade. As Luc Lang put it: 'If representation can no longer appear in painting without a reference to photography, then Richter will paint a photographed world.'[8] In Richter's work, the photograph's character as an indexical sign works to provide him with a kind of 'visual indifference' or anti-composition.[9] Richter makes paintings of photographs as pictures of paintings. In employing photography to make readymade paintings, Richter is deemed to have emptied out many of the claims of the modernist legacy: organic plenitude gives way to blankness; and the claims of the expressive subject are hollowed out as the trace of the artist's hand gives way to the trace of the apparatus. It is significant for my argument that Richter's photo-paintings are frequently deemed to have 'mechanised' the subject of painting, working in and against the process of reification. Osborne's account of the utopian remainder in Richter's work is worth noting here because, although he doesn't quite put it like this, he attaches Adorno's categories of the 'mimetic' and the 'cognitive' to the distinct poles of the photo-painting.[10]

What is left unexplored in these accounts of recent art is why some values and attributes should have settled on the photograph's indexical relation to its object. A few questions suggest themselves from the examples I have just introduced: Why it is that vernacular pictures are deemed to exist in the indexical register? Why does the photograph's status as indexical sign remove it from the condition 'of art'? Why does Wall associate these terms with the 'working class' and the 'lower-middle class', 'suburbanites', and the rest? Why does Buchloh equate the indexical form with the 'mechanical', or Osborne set painting's cognitive function against it? The instances can be multiplied almost indefinitely, but it is notable that in all of these accounts the photograph, seemingly because it bears an indexical relation to its model, is perceived as a low form. I want to argue that the ontological condition of the indexical sign does not in itself explain why the photographic document seemingly escapes the orbit 'of art'. In order to understand this gravitational wobble in the status of the photographic document, it is necessary to reposition these theoretical debates in the *longue durée* of photography's figural patterns. In doing so, I do not want to reject the idea that photographs should be seen as indexical signs, rather I want to consider how history coagulates around this sign function.[11] To paraphrase Volosinov, the indexical sign needs to be viewed as 'an arena of the class struggle.'[12] I am going to focus this idea through a moment in the 1860s in Britain, when the contradictions of painting and photography were played out around questions of colour. This strange version of Richter in reverse gear has cast its long shadow over the histories of photography.

Whatever else they might have disagreed about, most nineteenth-century commentators on photography conceded that it had at least one significant draw back: It lacked colour. One writer quoted the dictum that, colouring was 'the sunshine of art, that clothes poverty in smiles, and renders the prospect of barrenness itself agreeable, while it heightens the interest, and doubles the charms of beauty'.[13] Despite this, he believed, the many 'illustrious pioneers of photography' had been unable to obtain a definite result in the reproduction of 'natural colours' by the camera. But, no doubt, because there was plenty of this 'poverty' about, photographers, he thought, needed to 'have recourse to the art of the painter'. This writer meant by this, that it was necessary to add colour to the photograph by hand. (See Figures 4-6) I am going to focus here

7 Wall's account, though, is built on some tendentious foundations. It can hardly be coincidental that his essay culminates in the argument that the failure of conceptual photography to escape the bounds of the 'Picture' resulted in the reintroduction of picturing into contemporary art.

8 Luc Lang, 'The Photographer's Hand: Phenomenology in Politics', in Jean-Philippe Antoine, Gertrud Koch, Luc Lang, *Gerhard Richter*, Dis Voir, 1995, p.34

9 For Richter and 'visual indifference' see Jean-Philippe Antoine, 'Photography, Painting and the Real: The Question of Landscape in the Painting of Gerhard Richter', ibid., p. 56

10 Osborne, 'Painting Negation: Gerhard Richter's Negatives', op. cit.

11 Peter Osborne presents a thorough philosophical account of the ontological status of the photographic sign in his recent essay 'Sign and Image', op. cit.

12 V.N. Volosinov, *Marxism and the Philosophy of Language*, Harvard University Press, 1986, p.23. For an attempt to explore Bakhtin/ Volosinov's idea in relation to photography see Jo Spence, 'The Sign as Site of Class Struggle: Reflections on Works by John Heartfield', *Block* No. 5, 1981, pp.2-13; and my 'The Machine's Dialogue', *Oxford Art Journal*, Vol. 13, No. 1, 1990, pp. 63-76

13 Anon., 'Lessons on Colouring Photographs', *The Photographic News*, November 26, 1858, p.138

14 Martell was the pseudonym of an American Dageurreotypist (Thomas Delf). Wall was probably the unrivalled English champion of photographic art during the middle of the nineteenth century.

15 Charles Martell, 'Colour In Its Relation to Photography', *The Photographic News,* published in twelve parts between June 1, 1860, and August 17, 1860. The citation is from the section published July 20, 1860, p.134

16 ibid.

17 John Barrell explores these debates in *The Political Theory of Painting From Reynolds to Hazlitt: 'The Body of the Public',* Yale University Press, 1986.

on two accounts of photography's relation to colour provided by Charles Martell and Alfred H. Wall.[14]

In his influential series of texts on photography and colour that appeared in *The Photographic News* in 1860, Martell argued that 'colouring photographs by artificial means does not come within the scope of these essays'.[15] Martell wanted to instruct photographers in the art of colour, in so far as this would help those operators with no artistic training to avoid acts of bad taste. He argued that outline, relief, and colour constituted the painter's three key resources. However, while outline was sufficient to convey the idea of an object, the representation of surfaces required light and shade. According to him, outline provided the foundation of art, because, without it, relief and colour were unbounded and there could be no true representation of objects. In this argument, outline is primary, relief of secondary significance, while colour occupies 'the lowest rank'. Martell claimed that outline was the only conventional form among the components of a picture because it did not exist in nature. He wrote that outline:

> *...speaks most to our intelligence, because it artificially delineates that which in every object first strikes the attention. In looking at Flaxman's Shield of Achilles, for instance, before remarking its colour, or the relief of the chiselling that embellishes it, we have already observed whether it be round or square... And this distinctive character – that first seized upon by the understanding – is not the relief, nor the colour, but the external contour, the outline and it is all-sufficient.*[16]

If Martell's argument might appear counter-intuitive to us it is because he, along with most other writers in the 1860s, was working with the legacy of academic art theory that despised any form of literalism. Academic thought, in contrast to the kinds of naturalism that have become associated with photography, valued *conventional* forms because they were deemed to be the products of the intellect rather than the work of 'mindless' copying.[17] Colour, Martell thought, was more closely related to feeling than to understanding, and it acted upon animals more than on humans because, he claimed, animals shared our feelings but lacked our intelligence. Colour was perceived by Martell to be both 'disposable' and 'supplementary'. It was, perhaps, lucky for the photographers of the 1860s that the academic hierarchy ran in this direction.

It ought to be a familiar enough argument by now that the idea of colour as a supplement – as 'mere' decoration – occupies a prominent place in the long history of art and aesthetics. At least since Plato, colour has been thought of as feminine: a superficial gilding applied to dress up and beautify the plain truth. Colour has typically been thought of as deceiving its (male) beholders. In the academic tradition, colour was predominantly counterposed to line, which was conceived as intellectual and masculine. While colour clearly

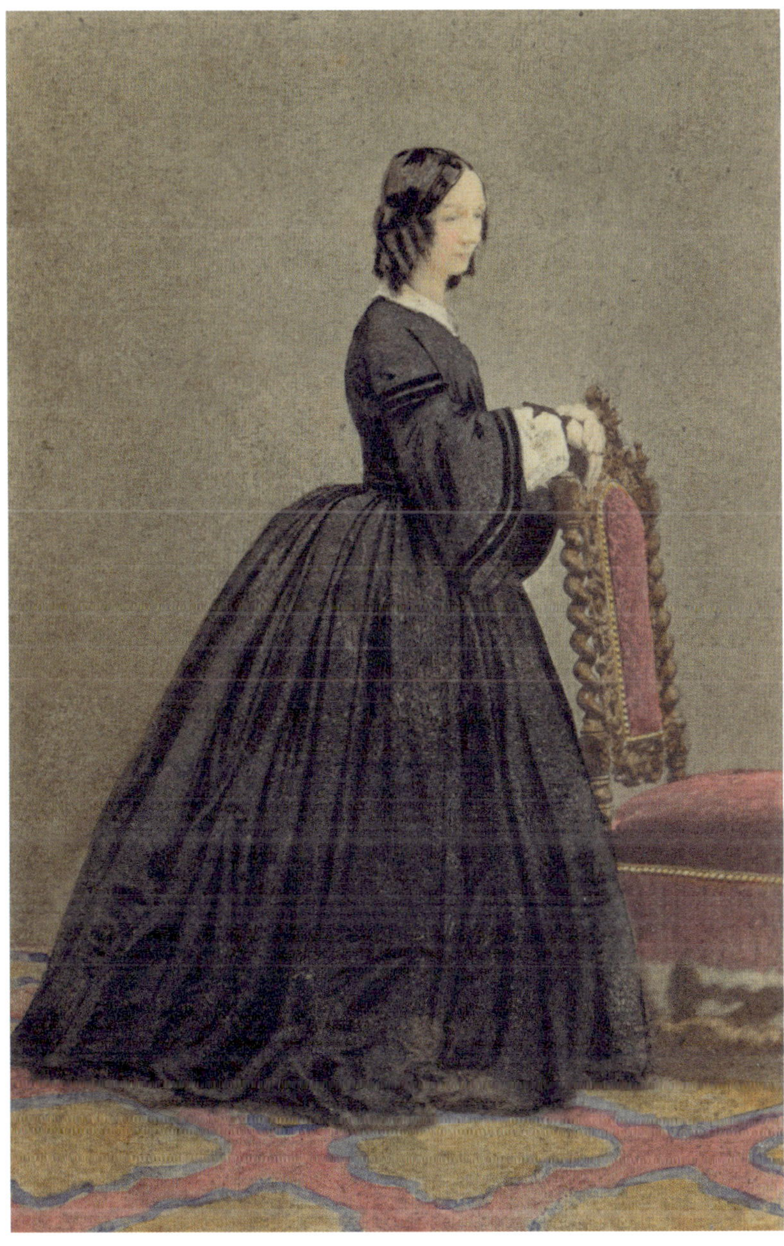

Figure 4. Photographer
unknown, *Portrait of a Woman,*
carte de visite, c.1870.

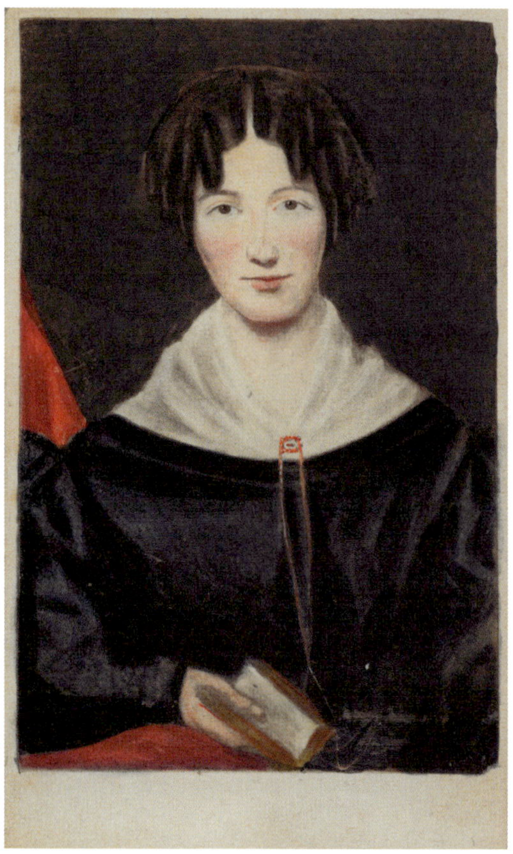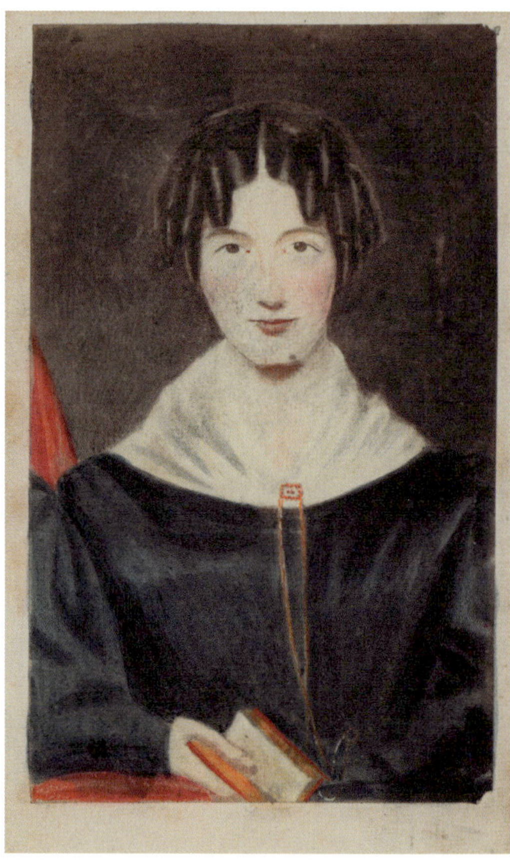

Figure 5. Photographer unknown, *Portrait of a Woman*, two cartes de visite, c.1870. .

18 Sir Joshua Reynolds, *Discourses on Art*, Yale University Press, 1975, Discourse IV, p.63.

occupied a gendered position in nineteenth-century art theory, it could also figure workers and artisans who were thought to be entranced by sensual pleasure of gaudy and showy display; colour was also related to the taste of so-called 'savages' whose alleged taste for bright things and body decoration was directly equated with lowly pleasures. According to Reynolds colour was an 'ornament' – a kind of afterthought – which embellished the intellectual force of a line. Colour, for him, was an inessential decorative feature – akin to luxury – and which appealed to the senses rather than the intellect. It is for this reason that Reynolds repeatedly affirmed the superiority of the Renaissance painters of Rome and Bologna over the Venetian masters. Tintoretto, Veronese and the Venetian school were, he said, 'more willing to dazzle than to affect', and to elevate the inferior and mechanical aspects of painting.[18] Critics of kitsch, the culture industry, or the Society of the Spectacle, need to pick their way through these figurative patterns with more care than has sometimes been in evidence.

Chiaroscuro, Martell continued, is the most 'difficult part of the painter's art', and not only in light and shade but also in colour. The absence of colour was, therefore, not to be so much regretted in photography as first imagined. This absence, he argued, was more than compensated for by the fact that 'In delineating all the delicate gradations and modifications of light and shade that constitute chiar-oscuro, photography stands pre-eminent'.[19] In defining photography in relation to chiaroscuro Martell cast it as an intellectual practice, or at least one equivalent to the Dutch and Flemish masters. If colour were to be added to photography it would, he suggested, be: 'the crowning glory of an art which, in its peculiar sphere, has, even now, no rival'. By claiming that photography centred on 'chiaroscuro and mathematically correct drawing' Martell was able to locate the practice in a pattern of figuration that cast it as high-born, masculine and European.

If Charles Martell felt that the actual colouring of photographs was beyond the scope of his essay – concerned as he was to educate photographers in the art of colour – Alfred H. Wall, in his *A Manual of Photographic Colouring*, was quite prepared to mix these two kinds of knowledge. In his text Wall offered a series of artistic aphorisms on colour. He supplied technical instructions on how to colour photographs and he provided some general remarks on the state of photographic colouring. We might be tempted to say that the specific object of Wall's account was the *painted photograph*. But we need to pause before making that snap judgement, since Wall revealed that his contemporaries found such a coupling of terms difficult to countenance. For the viewers of the 1860s the terms – painting and photograph – could not be made to settle long enough in the same space to make sense. Wall stated the problem forthrightly:

> *Coloured photographs occupy an undeservedly questionable situation: the artist curls his lip at them, because, as he says, they are not paintings; and the photographer sneers at them, because, as he says, they are not photographs. They are peremptorily denied admittance to galleries of paintings, and it is continuously and frequently urged that they should not be admitted to photographic exhibitions. Why, then, is this poor art to be an outcast among its brethren, unacknowledged and denounced by both artists and photographers?* [20]

If the photograph has been described as a bastard in the family of art, the painted photograph might properly be described as a foundling since, according to Wall, all parties left it on someone else's doorstep. According to Wall:

> *...[the] photographer admits the beauty of colour in a painting, and admires it as warmly as need be. The artist admits the truthfulness of the photograph, and*

19 Charles Martell, 'Colour In its Relation to Photography', *The Photographic News*, June 1, 1860, p.50.

20 Alfred H. Wall, *A Manual of Artistic Colouring as Applied to Photography. A Practical Guide to Artists and Photographers. Containing Clear, Simple, & Complete Instructions for Colouring Photographs on Glass, Paper, Ivory, & Canvas, With Crayon, Powder, Oil, or Water Colours. With Chapters on the Proper Lighting, Posing, and Artistic Treatment Generally of Photographic Portraits; and on Colouring Photographic Landscapes*, Thomas Piper, 1861, p.3

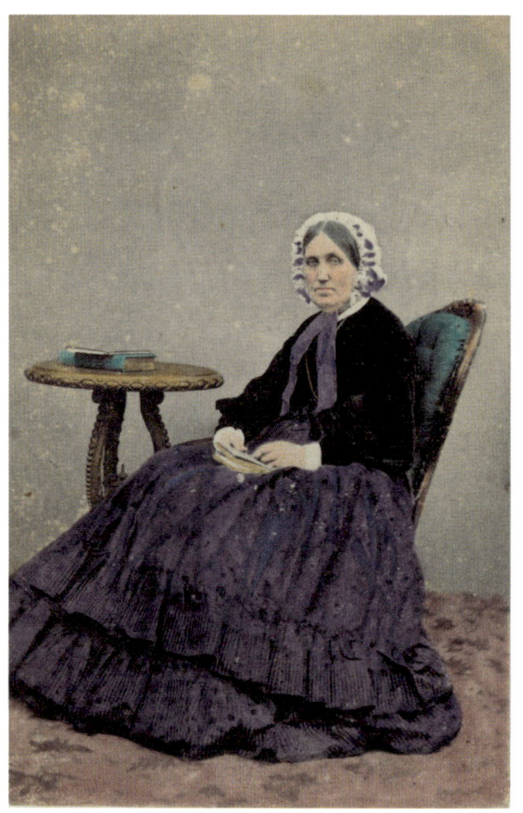

Figure 6. Mason and Co., London, *Portrait of a Woman*, carte de visite.

21 ibid.

22 ibid.

23 Fred Orton, *Flag*, Television programme for the course A316, Modern Art: Practices and Debates, The Open University/B.B.C, 1993. See also the same author's *Figuring Jasper Johns*, Reaktion Books, 1994

admires its wondrous delicacy of detail, faithfulness of drawing, and perfection of chiaroscuro just as warmly. Why, then, should an art which combines the truth of the one with the loveliness of the other be thus unsparingly denounced by these two important classes?[21]

Clearly Wall felt that the addition of paint to the photograph positioned the image outside the established categories of knowledge. This strange, hybrid representation belonged neither to the world of art nor to that of the utilitarian document. The 'coloured photograph' was, he claimed, a 'pariah in the world of art'.[22]

Probably the best way to account for the coloured photograph's odd status as artistic 'pariah' is to echo Fred Orton's important work on Jasper Johns.[23] Paraphrasing Orton, we could say that the painted photograph was a painting,

albeit photographed: or else it was a photograph, but painted. It was not a
painting because it was photographed, and it could not be a photograph
because it was painted. It was both a photograph and a painting, and it was
neither a photograph nor a painting. It was a painted photograph, or a photograph painted – which is to say that it was nothing. The painted photograph
was an object defying definition, which could be described as an undecidable
term or aporia. What interests me here is the way that the problem of the
painted photograph of the 1860s can so easily be stated in the terms that
Orton set out for unpacking John's neo-Duchampian art. The difference
between the painted photographs of the 1860s and Orton's account of *Flag*
turns on aporia. If I have introduced the idea of the painted photograph as
an aporia it is only to make it clear that I do not think that this is the correct
categorisation of these weird little pictures. There are, to be sure, no easy
answers to be found to this riddle of the coloured photograph, but there are
some clues and some vantage points from which to begin our search: these
turn on, what I call, 'allegories of labour'.[24]

If the absence of colour could be used to pull the photograph clear of its
lowly status, the persistent metaphor of the 'mechanical' that runs through
these texts exerts a gravitational force in the opposite direction. We should be
clear here: the term mechanical does not apply to the apparatus, the reference
in this literature is not to a machine but to a 'mechanic' or artisan. The term
mechanical copy, repeated *ad nauseum* in nineteenth-century writings on
photography, designated a process of literal inscription where 'hands' were
thought – at least by middle-class observers – to operate without intelligence
or mind. Mechanics copied the work of others, they did not invent, and this is
why photographs were deemed to be mechanical. What was being suggested
in such accounts of photography was that the photographic copy (or the
photographic sign in its indexical register) was like a worker. In later writing
on photography these two different senses of the term – apparatus on the one
side and the supposedly mindless mechanic on the other – got folded into one
another: their connotations then became vague and misty. During the 1860s,
though, the idea of the document as a literal copy – that is as an indexical
sign or 'proper' term – located the photographic image in a tropology of the
'motley proletariat'.

Some of the most interesting works of recent social theory – Jacques
Rancière's *On the Shores of Politics* or Michael Hardt and Antonio Negri's
Empire, for example – have returned to issues of class and universalism that
have been off the agenda for some time.[25] Here, however, I want to take
up Peter Linebaugh and Marcus Rediker's account of these issues because
their notion of the 'motley proletariat' is, I believe, particularly suited to the

24 See my forthcoming
*Allegories of Labour, Stories from
the Archives of Photography*.

25 Jacques Rancière, *On the
Shores of Politics*, Verso, 1995;
Michael Hardt and Antonio
Negri, Empire, Harvard
University Press, 2000; see also
Judith Butler, Ernesto Laclau
and Slavoj Zizek, *Contingency,
Hegemony, Universality:
Contemporary Dialogues on
the Left*, Verso, 2000.

26 Peter Linebaugh and Marcus Rediker, *The Many-Headed Hydra: The Hidden History of the Revolutionary Atlantic,* Verso, 2000.

27 Leader, 'Art Photography and Its Critics', *The Photographic News*, February 6, 1863, p.61. The hewers of wood and drawers of water are discussed in Linebaugh and Rediker, op. cit., pp.43-60; passim.; for the Hydra reference see Alfred H. Wall, 'Photography as Imitative Art', *The Photographic News*, November 9, 1860, p.327; Alfred H. Wall, 'In Search of Truth', *The British Journal of Photography*, July 15, 1863, p.285.

28 H.P.Robinson, *Pictorial Effect in Photography: Being Hints on Composition and Chiaroscuro for Photographers,* Piper and Carter, 1869, Helios reprint, 1971, p.60. This work first appeared as a series in *The Photographic News* during 1868.

29 ibid., pp.58-9.

30 Irish comrades should not feel too distressed by their absence from his list, I'm sure that this apparent exemption was just an oversight on Robinson's part.

historical work of unpicking photography's figural patterns.[26] In their book, *The Many-Headed Hydra,* Linebaugh and Rediker argue that at the moment of its creation the Atlantic working class was black and white (and every other colour imaginable), it was male and female, (it was queer and straight). It was cosmopolitan, open and democratic. *The Many-Headed Hydra* provides a way of unifying the oppressed and exploited under a category that is, from the outset, internally differentiated. This unity may be figural, but it is a category that is much more identifiable than Negri and Hardt's 'multitude'. The motley crew discovered a common ground, described in *The Many-Headed Hydra* as a 'universalism from below', in which terms like 'white' depended on social position rather than skin colour. The language of nineteenth-century photographic theory directly paralleled the terms of the motley proletariat, but it refracted them through a 'universalism from above': this is to say that the designation of the mob was attached to the indexical character of photographic signs. It is particularly striking, for instance, to find the practices of the document that were historically associated with the indexical sign equated with the 'hewers of wood and drawers of water', a phrase which, since the seventeenth century, has been used to designate indentured and unfree labour; or to discover the champions of photographic art casting themselves as Hercules slaying the Hydra of mechanical copying.[27] Here the indexical sign, at least for the champions of photographic art, figured misrule and mob violence.

In his book *Pictorial Effect in Photography,* H.P. Robinson, railed against photographic copyists who, he claimed, believed 'nature must be slavishly imitated, whether that nature be a pig-style or a palace...'.[28] According to Robinson, if the advocates of what he labelled the 'matter-of-fact' 'doctrine' were given free reign, then art would be 'no more than a servile copying of nature'. If this were to happen, he claimed, the works of photographers would be reduced to 'one dead level'. In this argument, Robinson set photographic-art against, what he called, 'common-place nature'.[29] In *Pictorial Effect*, servants, slaves, and levellers were all brought together in three pages under the identity of the copy-indexical sign.[30] What is significant here is the way that the indexical sign drew these figurations into the orbit of the photographic document. Another way of putting this is to say that in its long history art was positioned in opposition to a (denigrated) central category called the copy, which photographs – because they bore the indexical imprint of their model – fitted extremely well. As it met the language of art, the photographic sign accrued an allegory of labour. In this sense, at least, figural and ontological categories are not mutually exclusive. This is what is meant by the claim that the indexical sign should be seen as 'an arena of the class struggle'. The necessary rider here is that one side in this struggle – the working class – has always been irreducibly motley.

At this point it is worth returning to A.H. Wall's argument because, he, better than anyone, was prepared to follow the twisted logic of the painted photograph. This time, a word of caution before we begin: Wall may have been one of the most foremost commentators on photography of his generation, but he was a 'failed man'. Wall failed not only as a painter but also as a photographer. He then took to painting photographic backgrounds, colouring photographic portraits, and writing photographic criticism to make a living. The resentment is there in his writing. He claimed:

The great drawback felt by the artist who sits down, as many artists now do, to convert a photograph into a painting, preserving the truthfulness and character of the one with all the added charms of the other, arises from the inartistic charms of the photograph itself. Force, breadth and relief are the qualities which the portrait painter is anxious to secure in the lighting of the sitter's head, while the photographer, on the contrary, is only desirous of so lighting his models as to obtain 'short exposures' and images in which the sitter's boots and the sitter's face are equally illuminated, equally distinct, and equally prominent.[31]

Photographers recognised, that is, that the punters wanted the likeness generated by the image's indexical imprint, and not Wall's arty, coloured conundrum. Employers in the photographic industry required that colourists forget about the *'beau ideal'* and simply colour photographs – as Wall put it – 'naturally, cleanly, and brightly'.

Wall's argument suggests that the indexical trace of the object remained an overriding presence in the final image. In this account, the coloured photograph appears as a fetish: painting over the image distanced the model that the indexical sign testified to (and with it the characterisation of the photographer as a mechanical labourer) but, through a chain of contiguity, the colouring always simultaneously recalled the threat. The paint on the surface of a photograph called to mind the lack beneath it. Wall had an ingenious response to this ideological anxiety. He claimed there was nothing illegitimate about painting on a photograph. After all, he said, Leonardo, Titian, and Raphael all painted on the *abozzo* (an initial sketch, or drawn armature, that was designed from the outset to receive colour). And the *abozzo*, for Wall, was 'neither more nor less than a warm toned photograph'.[32] Or, to make the point more insistently, the photograph was an *abozzo*, since it was, Wall explicitly stated, a 'drawing'.[33] To which we could add, that it was always destined to be completed by the hand of the colourist.

As a commentator in *The Photographic News* suggested, there were two views as to the colouring of the photograph. On the one hand, there were the

31 A.H.Wall, in J.S. Templeton & A.W.Wall [sic], *The Guide to Miniature Painting and Colouring Photographs With a Few Words on Portrait painting in Water Colours*, George Rowney and Sons, 1865 (6th edition), p.48.

32 Wall, *A Manual of Artistic Colouring*, op. cit., p.2.

33 ibid., p.6.

photographers who believed their images to be complete; on the other hand,
there were the professional artists – and the professional photographic
colourists – who saw the photograph simply as a base on which to paint.
These two distinct groups often had very different conceptions of what made
a good photograph. While the former – professional photographers – felt their
photograph merely required 'the addition of colour in its most simple and
transparent form' (a practice more strictly referred to as tinting rather than
colouring), the latter – colourists – preferred, if they could get them, much
less dense images. Photographic colourists were inclined to see photographs
as sketches or drawings.[34]

34 'Lessons on Colouring',
The Photographic News
March 11, 1859, p.5.

Wall and Martell, for all their apparent differences, shared a conception:
they both believed that it was as an outline for colour that a photograph could
finally be redeemed as art. Their argument was not about the literal appearance
of paint on the surface of the image: it was not a claim about the painted
photograph *resembling a painting*. Rather, their argument seems to have been
that, as a consequence of painting over the image the photograph could be
envisaged as a drawing. In this odd way, photographs could come to occupy
the status held by line in academic theory. Painting on the photograph was,
for Wall and Martell, inessential and essential in equal measure: it took the
application of colour to sever the photograph's causal connection to its model.
This was a shift in perception generated out of the language of art. As we have
seen, in the academic theory of painting the terms line and colour held very
determinate weights. In an artistic culture still under the shadow of Reynolds,
elevating line over colour amounted to claiming the high terrain. Through this
convoluted argument Wall and Martell's advocacy of photographic colouring –
which at first sight appeared to cast the image as mechanical, feminine and
servile – could be used to draw the photograph away from those allegorical terms
rotating around its indexical register. The intellectual status of the photograph
turned on acknowledged artistic hierarchies of colour and line (even if, or
because, the colouring itself was so botched). Submerged under layers of
paint, the photograph could finally appear as art in the form of a drawing: as
figured rather than proper. The brute facticity of the photograph, its Barthesian
presence, could, thereby, be kept at bay. In this paradoxical moment of craft,
which emphasised the hand at the expense of the apparatus, a gap seemed to
open up in which the claims of the intellect might be asserted. But winning
access to the realm of art in this fashion came at a high price: This victory
of photography as art was bought at the cost of photography's very negation.
Wall and Martell were able to construct an argument that enabled the
photograph to be admitted to the citadel of art, but its literal disappearance
was a requirement for this move. The photograph, then, could be imagined

without the indexical presence of the model – that is to say it could take its
distance from copying (and all its associations of mechanical labour) – so
long as it did not exist. Submerged under layers of paint, the dead-weight of
negative figuration could be forgotten, and the petty-bourgeois subject could
proclaim his freedom.[35] The photograph's invisibility was a condition for its
existence as art.

It will come as no surprise for me to say that this was an unstable settlement.
The academic champions of photography were always bound to encounter
a problem since the public audience for whom Reynolds had written the
Discourses had given way to a very different establishment. The significant
point here is not simply that the language of political economy had eroded the
constituencies for academic criticism, but that the imbrication of photography
in social practice produced a series of shifting audiences. If we temporarily
pull apart the terms painting and photograph we will find two unrecognisable
accounts of the world: one deemed elevated and intelligent, the other stupid
and vulgar. Wall could not quite help admitting just this. And so he conceded
the status of the photographic colourist was precarious at best because: 'The
market is full of inferior colourists, who jostle and elbow each other at every
turn; and these are working at such absurdly low prices, that a decent livelihood is, for such, almost out of the question'.[36]

Wall, perhaps because he was so intent on raising the standing of photography, on various occasions, punctured his narrative with some economic
realities. In this instance, he warned against the danger of 'advertising quacks'
who claimed to be able to teach colouring in only a handful of lessons. As he
put it:

*Several young persons of either sex, anxious to secure a genteel if humble
livelihood, have, to my personal knowledge, been induced by such deceptive
advertisements to expend their little all in procuring materials and lessons,
and in supporting themselves while studying, only to find at the expiration of
the lessons, that, while quite unable to earn a shilling by the information thus
acquired, and without means of support, they were placed at the mercy of their
friends and acquaintances, or of the cold hard world... in one case, a most
respectable young lady was thus victimized, and plunged into the most terrible
dangers and difficulties.[37]*

This is no longer the language of academic art but is closer to that of the social
surveys that take as their object distressed needlewomen, or the dangers faced
by the impoverished governess. There are plenty of other examples of instances
were the political unconscious of photography was split open by the material
realities of commercial portrait practice. All the same, the account of the painted
photograph produced by Wall and Martell reads like a strange premonition.

35 This same logic can be seen
in reverse in the debates on
the practice of retouching in
The Photographic News for 1871
and 1872. This was the period –
1869-1871 to be exact – which
Rejlander described as 'the
years of photographic falsehood'
due to the demand for
retouching (cited in
[George Wharton Simpson],
'Retouching: its Use and
Abuse', *The Photographic News*,
September 29, 1871, p.460). In
this article Simpson bemoaned
the increasing 'sophistication'
of photography and sought to
reaffirm the direct truth of the
unsophisticated image.
Simpson claimed the image
became mechanical when it
departed from truth – a claim
that required the blending of
different aesthetic traditions.
Most contributors recognised
that retouching could not be
entirely dispensed with – the
pragmatics of the market would
not allow for that – and argued
it should be strictly limited to
altering flaws in the negative
and temporary blemishes such
as spots or freckles on the skin.
Interestingly, it was also felt
that scars could be removed or
reduced without affecting the
truth of the image, no doubt
because they departed from
ideal likeness. As I have said,
in its essentials, this debate
followed the same logic as Wall
and Martell to the effect that
drawing on the image
distanced it from the stupid
and insensible impression of
the apparatus. The difference
was that while Wall and Martell
took this to be an unconditional
good, the contributors to the

debate on retouching were considerably more troubled by handwork. There is enough material in the journals to work up a substantial argument on the truth content of the document and retouching; but given the close parallel to the argument on colour I have elected not to pursue this part of the dialectical movement. In addition to the essay by Simpson the most interesting contributions are: [George Wharton Simpson], 'Retouching and Photographic Truth', *The Photographic News*, January 19, 1872, pp.25-26; Edwin Cocking, 'Art and Truth in Photography', *The Photographic News*, January 19, 1872, p.29; George Croughton, 'Photographic versus Literal Truth', *The Photographic News*, January 19, 1872, pp.30-32; H. P. Robinson, 'Retouching and Exhibitions', *The Photographic News*, January 26, 1872, pp.41-42. The numbers of these texts, which appear in the same issue, suggest that their origin was in the discussion, which followed Croughton's paper at the South London Photographic Society.

36 Wall, *A Manual of Photographic Colouring,* op. cit., p.4.

37 ibid., pp.4-5.

Throughout the twentieth century there have been repeated attempts to secure photography on the grounds of art. But – for the Pictorialists, or those at *Aperture,* or in New York's MoMA's photography department – the document (or copy, or proper term, or indexical imprint of the model) has always played havoc with this desire. When photography finally did find a way into the institutions of art it was again through a confrontation with painting. In this sense, the work of Rauschenberg and Warhol, Richter and Celmins, Ruscha, Close and others, can be seen to have performed the task of a vanishing mediator for the institutionalisation of photography. It should be observed that in this body of work, as with the painted photograph of the 1860s, the condition for photography's emergence as art was its literal disappearance. Recent commentators on the contemporary practice of photo-painting are right to see it as a practice of ironisation that problematises both terms: the photograph is stripped from representation and yet retains it; the painting is made over as image while maintaining a distance from it.

What I would want to add to this argument is that the conditions for this project also depend on the figural patterns of the motley proletariat that have coagulated around the photographic pole of the photo-painting. The point is not just that these are 'high and low' categories, but that the photographic document as a low term is saturated with academic theory's maidservants, slaves and workers. All are deemed mindless and, in the absence of mind, they are figured as literal. In the nineteenth century the status of art photography turned on marking its distance from this figural clustering; in our time, art still requires the indexical photographic sign to be distanced through irony, often by painting over it, or by redoing it by hand. Far from having disappeared this cluster of tropes continues to haunt photography: the trace of the model apparent in the image continues to draw to itself the figurative patterns of the motley proletariat, even if they now appear merely as pale shadows.

I conclude with an image that recapitulates the strange haunted nature of photography: John Baldassari's *The Artist is Not Merely The Slavish Announcer Of A Series of Facts, Which In This Case The Camera Has Had To Accept and Mechanically Record* of 1966-68. (Figure 7) In this work Baldassari combines both the indexical sign in its low vernacular form (amateur blocking of sight-lines, misaligning of objects, and splitting of the frame), with a text that contains two of the central categories of photography's long figural history in, and through, the motley proletariat. In this work photography is yet again, 'mechanical' and 'slavish' (Baldassari seems to have missed the gendered moment of the maidservant). Whether consciously or as historical remainder, Baldassari's 'painting' encapsulates the histories of photography as they rotate around the indexical imprint of the model: high and low, art and document,

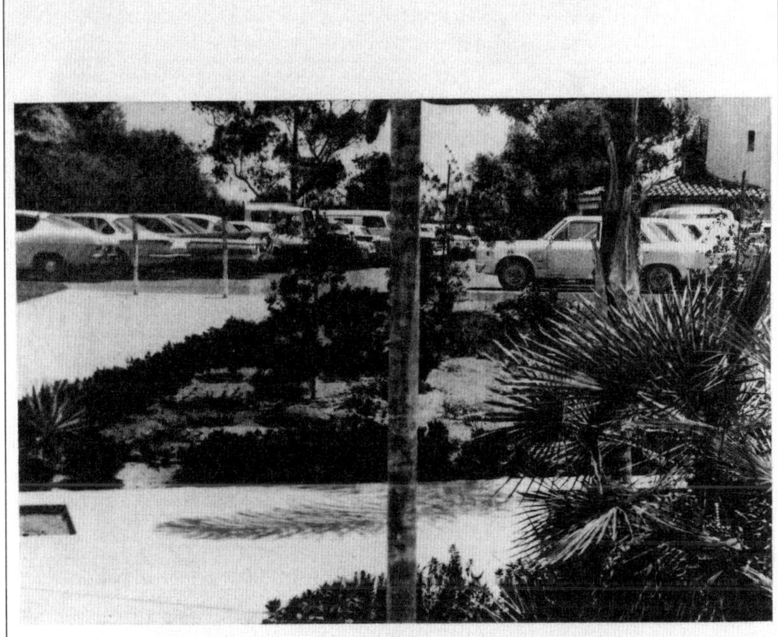

Figure 7. John Baldassari, *The Artist is Not Merely The Slavish Announcer Of A Series of Facts, Which In This Case The Camera Has Had To Accept and Mechanically Record*, 1966-68.

picture and copy, pictorial and vernacular, figured and literal, brain and hand, middle class and worker, masculine and feminine, black and white... .
Another way of describing the histories of photography would be to say that they are generated out of this fusion between the categories of academic aesthetics and the ontological condition of the indexical sign. Yet another way to put this would be to say that photography exists in the space of allegory.

From presence to the performative:
rethinking photographic indexicality
David Green and Joanna Lowry

Undoubtedly one of the most important issues in discussions about photography in the past decade has been concerned with the implications of electronic and digital technologies for traditional chemically-based photographic practices. Beginning in the late 1980s and gathering momentum with the increasing availability of these new technologies, the force of critical opinion has lain largely with those who – believing that the medium's privileged status as an arbiter of truth and measure of reality had been fatally undermined by computerised imaging processes – have sought to reconcile us to the 'death of photography'. Yet, paradoxically, during this same period we have also witnessed a fascination amongst a younger generation of photographers with precisely those qualities and values associated with the medium that have been deemed most at risk and which has led to the attempt to recuperate that particular engagement with reality that photography seems to offer. Both of these phenomena are, of course, related to each other. They each pose a set of problems around how we construe photography's relationship to the real, and about the relationship between our reading of the photographic image and our understanding of the technologies that helped to produce that image. At the heart of these issues lies the question of the photograph's indexicality.

In any discussion about indexicality and photography the impact of Roland Barthes' *Camera Lucida* cannot be underestimated. Yet the influence of this text has had, we would argue, a subtly distorting effect on our understanding of the nature of photographic indexicality. Centred on a reading of a photograph of the writer's dead mother it has led, inevitably, to a preoccupation with the origins of the photographic image in a chemical trace, to its relationship with time and absence, and to the complexity of our affective response when we encounter this evidence of a moment that has passed. As a result discussions about the index seem to have gained particular significance because of the way in which they have contributed to a wider set of cultural discourses concerning the relationships between photography, memory, death and mourning.

However, we want to argue here that the concept of the photograph as a trace of a past event does not exhaust our understanding of its indexical properties. Indeed, it was C.S. Peirce – to whom we owe the earliest and still most thorough analysis of indexicality – who demonstrated that the indexical sign was less to do with its causal origins and more to do with the way in which it pointed to the event of its own inscription. Photographs, therefore, are not just indexical because light happened to be recorded in an instant on a piece of photosensitive film, but because, first and foremost, they were taken. The very act of photography, as a kind of performative gesture which points to an event in the world, as a form of designation that draws reality into the image field, is thus itself a form of indexicality.

These two forms of indexicality, the one existing as a physical trace of an event, the other as performative gesture that points towards it, both invoke a relationship to the real that seems to be specific to the photographic image. In this essay we would like to look more closely at the relationship between these two aspects of the photographic for it seems to us that, while each of them promises a kind of security in their relationship to the real, they also simultaneously subvert that security and challenge our commitment to it.

Amongst the first to draw attention to these issues were not photographic theorists but those artists engaged in conceptual practices in the later 1960s and early 1970s for whom photography played a key role in articulating a range of questions about the nature of the work of art and the status of its documentation. In his essay *"Marks Of Indifference": Aspects Of Photography In, Or As, Conceptual Art,* Jeff Wall argues that conceptual art's turn to photography represents a curious pursuit of a modernist ideal of the self-reflexivity of the medium in the attempt to locate its defining characteristics.[1] For photography this inevitably meant observance of its recording and evidential functions, its innate capacity for the depiction of things. Thus it is, Wall argues, that conceptual art comes to engage with a photojournalistic tradition of photography as reportage. The immediate precedent for this use by artists of photography-as-documentation would appear to lie with Ed Ruscha's series of photo-books beginning in 1963 with *Twenty-six Gasoline Stations* (Figure 8). Like the self-explanatory *Every Building on Sunset Strip, Los Angeles* (1966), this collection of photographs of every gasoline station along the route taken by the artist between Los Angeles and his parent's home in Oklahoma, is the result of a systematic process of visual documentation, decided in advance and seemingly executed without regard to artistic considerations. Whilst Ruscha's choice of subject matter relates closely to the contemporary interests of Pop artists in the vernacular and the everyday, his decision to present the work as straight photographic reproductions locates it as seminal in the pre-history of conceptual art. However, as Wall makes clear, what seems to have been made possible by Ruscha's example was less to do

1 Jeff Wall in Ann Goldstein and Anne Rorimer (eds), *Reconsidering the Object of Art: 1965-1975,* The Museum of Contemporary Art, Los Angeles and MIT Press, Mass., 1996.

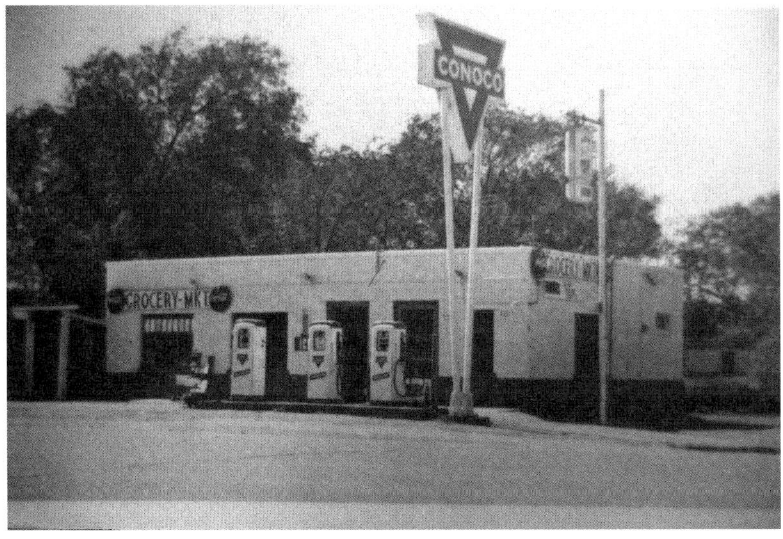

Figure 8. Ed Ruscha, 'Conoco, Saurg, Oklahoma' from *Twentysix Gasoline Stations,* 1963.

with presenting photographic documentation as art and more to do with a self-conscious 'parody' of the photograph's use as record.

Indeed the full implications of conceptual art's use of photography have nearly always been obscured, and its value underestimated, by positioning it firmly and simply in the realm of documentation. It is clear, however, that conceptual artists, rather than blithely accepting the notion of documentation, subjected it to either a kind of playful critique or to forms of wholesale deconstruction. In the case of the former, artists such as Douglas Heubler used photography within a normative system for structuring and ordering information but undermined its function as documentation by simply applying it to phenomena of the utmost triviality. As regards the latter – in the early works of John Hilliard and Jan Dibbets, for example – strategies involving the systematic investigation of the technical parameters of the medium exposed the tenuous hold that the photograph has over the real and the instability inscribed in the very notion of the photograph as an objective record. In more general terms it can be seen that, if photography played a key role in conceptualism's aim of problematising dominant notions of art and the art object, it did not simply provide a means by which this process was to be 'documented' but actually provided the actual arena in which it was to be acted out. Furthermore, the photographs themselves were not merely the residue of that process but constituted its actual realisation. In pointing to this complex interdependency

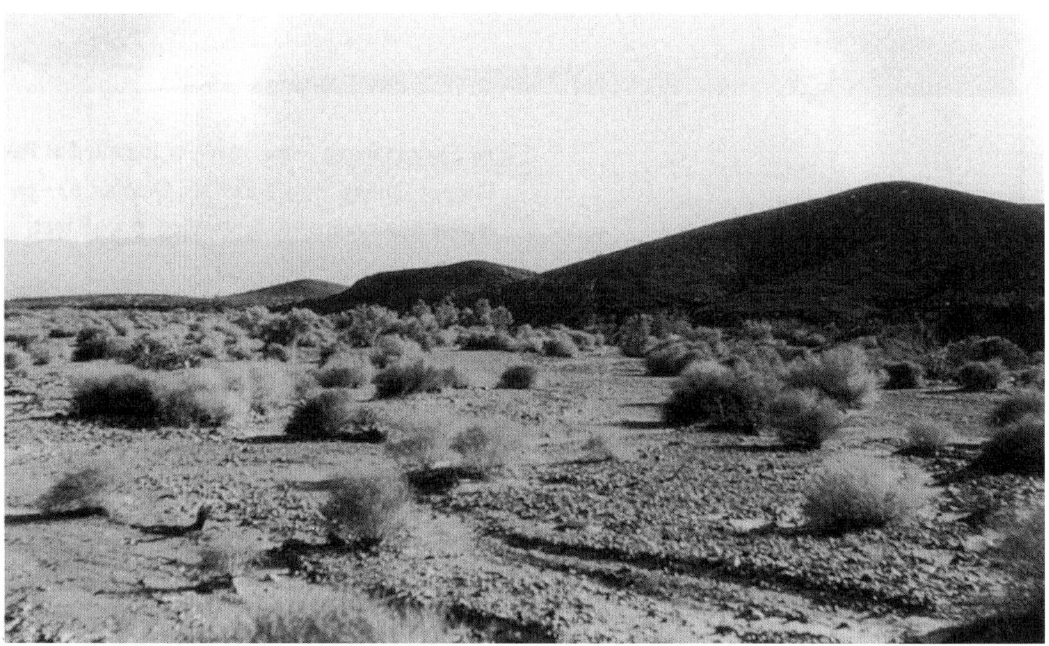

between an event and its record, conceptual artists drew attention to the twinned aspects of indexicality that are fundamental to photography itself.

Nowhere is this point made more clearly than in a series of photographs made by Robert Barry in 1969 entitled the *Inert Gas Series* (Figure 9). This consists of a number of photographs and accompanying text which detail the artist's actions of releasing various invisible gases in specific locations around Los Angeles. The photographs purport to show these events but, of course, nothing can be seen other than the actual settings – a barren patch of desert, an isolated beach, a empty park and so on – to verify the claims made on behalf of the image by the accompanying text. Barry's production of a photographic record of these non-visible works of art might seem consciously futile and absurd yet these images may be significant for our understanding of the limitations of a particular form of indexical inscription. If at one level these images are displayed as documentary evidence denoting a state of affairs, what is also clear is that they are carefully designed to be at the limit point of photography's documentary capacity. While providing us with the indexical trace of the moment of the gas's release they also gesture towards the impossibility of recording it, and our attention shifts instead towards the act of photography itself as the moment of authentication. Thus the photograph is not intended so much to denote the inert gas that cannot be seen as to point us towards it, and in that process of pointing to declare its existence. The intended effect of the photographic statement is to produce our belief in the existence of this invisible phenomenon, rather than simply to witness it being there. However, in order for such an act to be effective, certain conditions have to have been fulfilled – the photograph has to be taken by or authenticated by the artist, the date and time have to have been recorded, its passage into the public domain has to be controlled by the artist and it has to be displayed in a particular way. If these social and discursive conditions are not in place then we may good reason to doubt the sincerity of what we are being presented with; hence the matter-of-fact rhetoric that accompanies the photograph as its extended title, such as: 'Krypton, from a measured volume to indefinite expansion. On March 3, 1969 in Beverly Hills, California, one litre of Krypton was returned to the atmosphere.'

One consequence of Barry's work is the way in which it directs us towards a problem in photography's relationship to the visual. There is an obvious discrepancy in the *Inert Gas Series* between that which is actually recorded in the photograph – the landscape settings in which the events took place – and that which is supposedly denoted by it – the release of the inert gas. The visual – what is actually recorded – is in an interesting way in excess of the intended significance of the photograph: it has, what we might call a 'supplementary' role in relationship to it. At the level of signification the visual is suppressed and yet it necessarily returns as a presence that – to quote Barthes – 'fills the field with force'. If at one level Barry's images can be seen as an ironic negation of modernism's insistence that works of art existed as things primarily to be looked at – in Michael Fried's terms, to be 'accessible to eyesight alone' – what is ultimately at stake in this work is that is poses the problem of visuality in a genuinely deconstructive manner. In particular, what the *Inert Gas Series* highlights for us is the inadequacy of the conventional theoretical frameworks that attempt to account for the operations of the photographic sign, primarily or exclusively, in terms of the image as an indexical trace, a residual presence of that which 'has been'. Instead what we recognise as important here is the photographic act itself and to understand this we need to think about how artists such as Barry were using photography 'performatively'.

The concept of the performative that we are drawing on here is one derived from speech act theory as it was developed by J.L. Austin in a series of lectures given in the mid 1950s and published in 1962 as *How to Do Things with Words*. Austin was preoccupied with certain aspects of language which he felt could not be accounted for by conventional philosophical theories of language which tended to focus in their analysis upon certain types of sentence known as 'constatives' – sentences which seemed to describe an event or matter of fact. The meaning of these statements was dependent upon their implicit denotative relationship to the real world and thereby to an implicit set of assumptions as to their truth-value. (We need only note here that there are obvious parallels between the way in which we think about these kinds of constative statements and the ways in which we commonly think about the photograph – as a special kind of sign that seems to picture or denote an event – and which is similarly embedded in a set of powerful ideas about its relationship to truth and the real). Austin, at first, contrasted constatives with a type of linguistic phenomenon whose meaning was not determined by this sense of a denotative relationship to the real world but which seemed instead to act upon the world, producing it, changing it. These linguistic phenomena, which Austin termed 'performatives' could best be interpreted as actions rather than being decoded as meanings. Beyond, therefore, the ways in which we make use of language to communicate information or make some statement about the world, we also use it to do things with: to ask questions, give orders, make promises, offer apologies and so on. The basic idea of what Austin termed 'speech acts' is that the act of saying something is at the same time doing what one says. A simple example would be that in saying 'I promise .... x, y, or z', the speaker is actually making a promise.

One significant aspect of Austin's exploration of the performative that we need to note for our purposes here is that, while his analysis begins with the very special cases of performatives in language, distinguishing them from constatives, he gradually begins to extend his analysis to include constatives themselves as very special cases of performatives – for example the statement 'the tree is in the garden' which might be assumed to be a constative describing a state of affairs is in fact, at a deeper level, a sort of truncated version of the performative declaration that 'there is a tree in the garden'. Thus Austin extends his analysis of these examples of a peculiar, particular, overlooked category of linguistic phenomena so that they come to tell us something profound about the nature of language itself. In this move he established in effect a whole shift in the debate around the ontology of language that was to have profound impact on both linguistics and philosophy in the second half of the twentieth century, locating language firmly in the social.[2] In conjunction with the later work of Wittgenstein who had similarly abandoned the attempt to discover truth through the analysis of linguistic statements and had encouraged us instead to look at the ways in which language was used by us to make things happen, Austin provided a radical means of deconstructing our assumptions about the relationship between the language and truth. For truth, from the perspective of speech act theory, would always ultimately be

2 This is not to ignore the seminal work of much earlier writers such as those associated with the Bakhtin school but the impact of that body of linguistic theory was only to be felt much later.

embedded within a set of social relationships, a type of contract entered into by language users.

Conceptual art in the late 1960s was influenced in a variety of ways by Anglo-American analytical philosophy – eclectically incorporating into its fold a range of different philosophical positions, ranging from logical postivism to ordinary language philosophy, from early to late Wittgenstein, and incorporating also discussions about speech act theory and performativity. The influence of Wittgenstein's writings, for example, were paramount in pre and early Art and Language work which, in the words of Terry Atkinson, was concerned with 'the business of pushing the idea of Duchamp's readymade to a point of cognitive exhaustion' by the use of a 'declarative strategy' that was usually textually based, whilst Joseph Kosuth had independently reached a similar position via a logical positivist theory of language which boiled down to his assertion that 'works of art are analytical propositions', to which he went to add in more prosaic terms that 'this is what [Donald] Judd means when he states 'if someone says his work is art, it's art''. Indeed in the period between about 1966 and 1970 it became a common concern to explore what possibilities existed in the idea of declaring, nominating, announcing, stating, claiming, identifying, reporting, that such and such a thing was a work of art. In retrospect in seems clear that whether that thing was a material object or whether it was merely an idea expressed in the form of a textual proposition was less important than the actual act of declaring, nominating, announcing, etc. In other words one of the most important strategies adopted by conceptual artists can be thought of as a form of speech act. (Whether that act carried what Austin called 'perlocutionary force' – that is whether anyone actually believed what they were saying – is, of course, another matter entirely.)

One artist who did draw directly on Austin's writings was Keith Arnatt. Undoubtedly the best known of Arnatt's early works – one might call it for obvious reasons his signature work – is *Trouser-Word Piece* which derives its title indirectly from the quotation from Austin's essay *Sense and Sensibilia* (Figure 10).[3] Arnatt had come across Austin's writings and those of other speech act theorists in the early 1960s and what he took from that experience was the notion that art could essentially be seen as a kind of action, or more specifically, as an act of utterance. More than that, however, what Arnatt seized upon were the consequences of art making as a performative utterance in shifting the notion of what an artist was and what he does. Put simply, the direct corollary of the conceptualist strategy of the declaration or nomination of any given material (or putatively immaterial) object as a work of art was that the status of artist assumed a different kind of institutional and discursive positionality. The identity of the artist, like the identity of the art object,

3 It is interesting to note that the photograph of Arnatt holding up a placard upon which he announces 'I'M A REAL ARTIST' has been often reproduced without the panel of text bearing the Austin quote that is meant to accompany it.

Keith Arnatt
TROUSER - WORD PIECE

'It is usually thought, and I dare say usually rightly thought, that what one might call the affirmative use of a term is basic - that, to understand 'x', we need to know what it is to be x, or to be an x, and that knowing this apprises us of what it is **not** to be x, not to be an x. But with 'real' .... it is the **negative** use that wears the trousers. That is, a definite sense attaches to the assertion that something is real, a real such-and-such, only in the light of a specific way in which it might be, or might have been, **not** real. 'A real duck' differs from the simple 'a duck' only in that it is used to exclude various ways of being not a real duck - but a dummy, a toy, a picture, a decoy, &c.; and moreover I don't know **just** how to take the assertion that it's a real duck unless I know **just** what, on that particular occasion, the speaker had it in mind to exclude .... (The) function of 'real' is not to contribute positively to the characterisation of anything, but to exclude possible ways of being **not** real - and these ways are both numerous for particular kinds of things, and liable to be quite different for things of different kinds. It is this identity of general function combined with immense diversity in specific applications which gives to the word 'real' the, at first sight, baffling feature of having neither one single 'meaning,' nor yet ambiguity, a number of different meanings.'
John Austin, 'Sense and Sensibilia.'

Figure 10. Keith Arnatt,
Trouser-Word Piece, 1972.

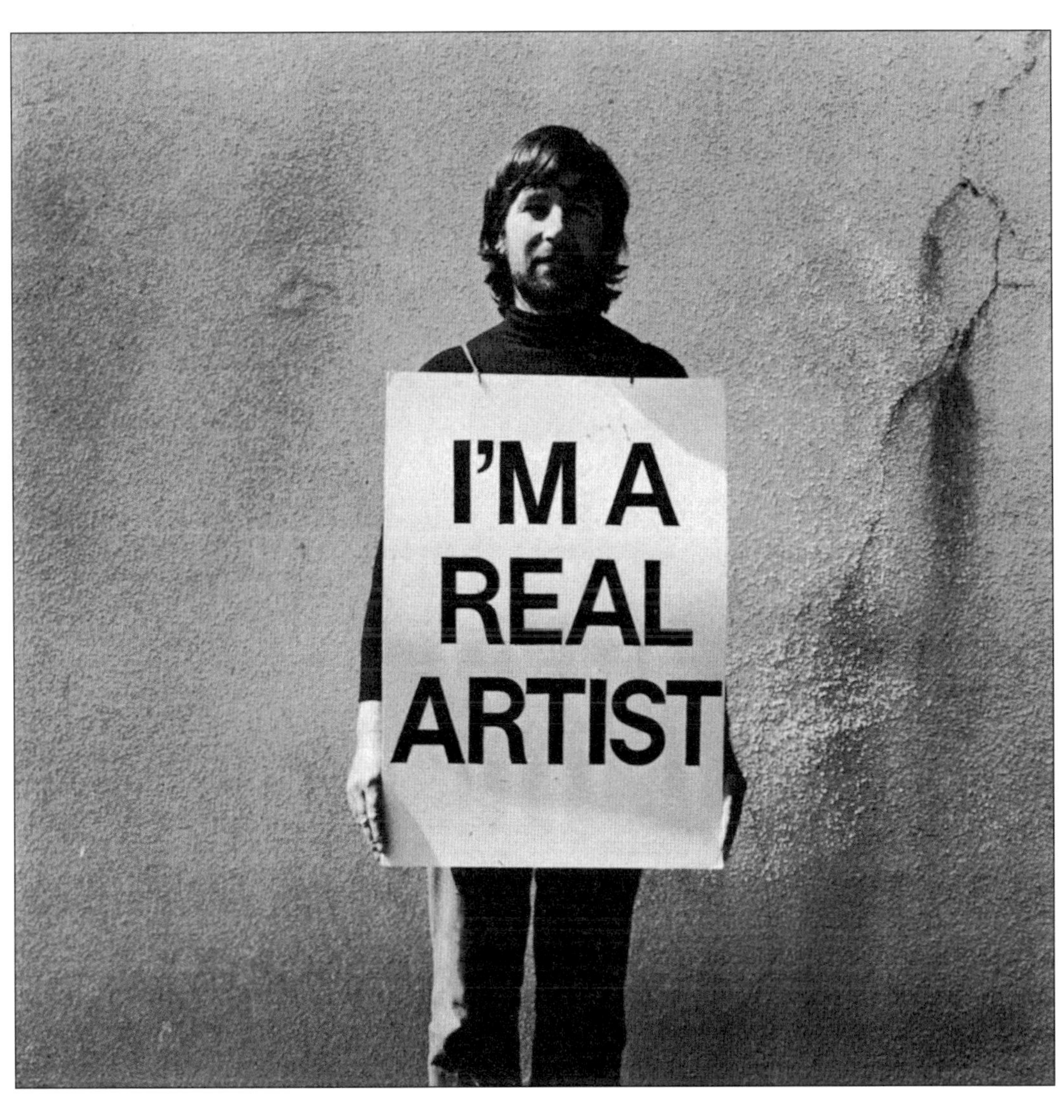

I'M A
REAL
ARTIST

becomes, in more senses than one, entirely nominal. This is nowhere more clearly registered than in another of Arnatt's pieces from this time, *Art and Egocentricity – A Perlocutionary Act?* (1972), which consists of a wall inscription that announces that 'KEITH ARNATT IS AN ARTIST' accompanied by a lengthy essay that sets out to analyse that declarative statement by means of speech act theory. What Arnatt sets out to do in that essay is to examine the notion of art as a presentation of the artist's intention and his right to nomination. Arnatt's reading of Austin, Searle and others allows him to recognise that saying something is a work of art, or saying that you are an artist, takes place within the complexity of the social contracts within which meaning and truth are formed.

It hardly needs pointing out that these two works by Arnatt function as performatives – although performatives disguised, as it were, as constatives – in the realm of language (entirely so in one case, partially so in the other). And it might be argued that, in the example of Robert Barry's work also, the declarative act is one embedded in the textual statement that accompanies the photographs, lending a kind of performativity to the role of anchorage that Barthes once identified as the structural relationship existing between the photograph and its accompanying caption.[4] However, we would argue that in an important sense these photographs *in themselves* resemble the structure of a speech act and that they do so precisely in terms of the complex interdependency between performatives and constatives, between socially defined utterances and truth statements, that Austin's work, almost despite himself, revealed. What we are therefore presented with in *Trouser-Word Piece* is not simply a photograph of Keith Arnatt but an image that is located within the genre of self-portraiture in which the role of the artist is performatively acted out. And, in a way that mirrors the convergence of the constative with the performative that Austin had once identified, we are faced in the *Inert Gas Series* with two forms of indexicality, coexisting within the same image: the first is that which presents itself as 'pure denotation', the trace of the scene of an event; the second is that of a gesture, an indicator that declares that the event is taking place.

An important consequence that flows from rethinking photographic indexicality in these terms is indicated in the uneasy juxtaposition of the two temporalities contained in the preceding sentence. We noted at the beginning of this essay that much of the discussion of photography's indexicality has been one that has been dominated by the gravitational force of Roland Barthes' seminal essay *Camera Lucida* in which – as Geoffrey Batchen observes elsewhere in this volume – the photograph seemingly becomes closely intertwined with a generalised sense of mourning, melancholia and loss. Yet, as anyone familiar

4 See Roland Barthes, 'Rhetoric of the Image' in *Image, Music, Text*, ed. S. Heath, Fontana, 1977.

with that essay – and more so with Barthes' earlier essays on photography – will know, this is a rather a crude and very partial characterization of his argument. For whilst, Barthes might stress an essential anteriority inscribed within the photograph, the overriding experience of the 'what has been', there is also the countervailing force that we see is also irrefutably and immediately 'present'. Whilst Barthes dealt with this fundamental paradox that the photograph presents us with in rather different ways, in essays written well over two decades apart, there is nonetheless an essential continuity to be observed here. For Barthes the enigma (or the magic) of the photograph lay within our experience of it as existing within two irreconcilable temporal frames that, as Ann Banfield has observed, confounded any attempt to find an equivalent in ordinary language. Banfield argues that the impossibility that Barthes faced in attempting to bring together what he described as 'an illogical conjuncture between the *here-now* and the *there-then*' might better be reformulated as: 'This was now here'.[5]

It would seem to us that this might be an appropriate way in which to describe the two kinds of indexicality that we have attempted to describe above as coexisting within the photograph: the one bound into the an ever receding past, the other occupying the horizon of a continual present. However, if the photograph can never escape its inevitable passage into history, marking as it does the irreversible flow of the present moment into the past, what we want to focus upon here is that equally insistent experiential factor of the photograph, which is that of the 'here and now'.

It was Peirce himself who noted that: 'The index has the being of present experience'[6], and ever since then it has fallen to both philosophers and linguistic theorists to dwell upon the ramifications of what he identified as one of the main classes of indices that he termed 'designators', those signs that only operate by reference to an object or event in the immediate spatio-temporal field. Whilst the terminology to describe such phenomena may vary – designation, ostention, indication are the most common forms of expression to be found – they are ultimately concerned with the same thing. This is what, (to settle on one term), linguists often refer to as deixis.[7] By this, is meant the form of everyday language behaviour in which meaning is inseparable from the physical context of the speaker's utterance. The most common type of deictics are those demonstrative, relative and personal pronouns (here, now, this, that, I, you, we, them) that only acquire meaning by being anchored in the specifics of time and space.

It will be obvious that our extension of the notion of the performative statement to include the photographic act is intended to foreground the idea of a gesture, a matter of pointing to something, that is similarly grounded in

5 Ann Banfield, 'L'imparfait de l'Objectif: the Imperfect of the Object G lass', *Camera Obscura*, 24, 1990, pp. 65-87. For a not dissimilar attempt to explore the irresolvable conjuncture of the past and the present within the photographic image with regard to Jan Dibbet's 'Perspective Correction' series see David Green, 'Between Object and Image', in *Creative Camera: 30 Years of Writing*, ed. D. Brittain, Manchester University Press, 1999, pp. 261- 268.

6 *Collected Papers of Charles Sanders Peirce*, eds. Charles Hartshorne, Paul Weiss and Arthur W. Burks, Cambridge, Mass., Harvard University Press, 1935-1966, Vol. 4, p.447.

7 Because of the overall drift of Barthes argument in *Camera Lucida*, it is easy to overlook the importance that he attaches to precisely this aspect of the photograph at the very beginning of his essay: 'Show your photographs to someone – he will immediately show you his: "Look," this is my brother; this is me as a child,"etc.; the Photograph is never anything but an antiphon of "Look," "See," "Here it is"; it points a finger at certain vis-à-vis, and cannot escape this pure deictic language.' Roland Barthes, *Camera Lucida*, trans. R. Howard, Hill and Wang, New York, 1981, p. 5.

the specificity of a particular time and place. Yet, what is important here is that in formulating the issue in these terms, we must avoid the trap of inadvertently reinstating the idea of the photographic document, that is as the truthful record of something that *has* happened. As we have tried to show in our brief discussion of conceptual art's use of photography, the intent seems to have been not to confirm but to ironise the documentary status of photography and what this involved was employing the photograph performatively to designate the real, rather than to represent it. Performativity, we are arguing, was central to the use made of photography by conceptual artists not so much for the fact that it provided the spectator with an indexical trace of the real through the recording of the event, but because it deictically invoked the real through 'pointing to' the event and, in effect, declaring it to be the case. The indeterminacy between these two forms of indexicality, far from confirming the status of the visible world, subtly puts it into question and draws our attention to the ways in which notions of the real are discursively produced.

As John Roberts has inferred – significantly for our purposes, within a discussion of conceptual art's use of photography – 'photography's powers of ostension' have often been overlooked; but also, and more importantly, that the importance of this property of the medium lies not so much with the mere fact of nomination but with what he calls it's 'inferential complexity', which we take to mean its claim upon description rather than just designation.[8] And this is precisely where contemporary photographers' preoccupations with the indexical nature of the photographic image seem to be relevant. There has been, in the last decade, a resurgence of interest in the use of photography to testify to our sense of the real. Perhaps the most insistent, or more self-conscious, trend has been towards configuring the 'real' in terms of the anti-social, even dystopic, character of various sub-cultural lifestyles. In the work of photographers such as Nan Goldin, Jack Pierson, Corinne Day, Jurgen Teller and Wolfgang Tillmans, the historically familiar tropes of realism – the everyday, the low and the mundane – are reworked through an iconography of the abject squalor and detritus of contemporary existence lived in a state of social and psychic restlessness. Seemingly consistent with this imagery is the language of rough-edged snapshot photography with all the signs of 'bad' photographic technique and deliberately displaying a form of amateurism that differs markedly from an early kind of 'anti-aesthetic' deployed by someone like Ruscha. Whilst this styleless-style might not be particularly original, its studied casualness befits the subjective, autobiographical and diaristic nature of such a practice, not least by the fact that it foregrounds the notion of personal testimony in the evidence of an embodied vision. Indeed it seems to us that what these often blurred, badly focused and ill-composed images seek to do above all is to

8 John Roberts, 'Photography, Iconophobia and the Ruins of Conceptual Art', in *The Impossible Document: Photography and Conceptual Art in Britain 1966-1976*, Camerawords, London, 1977.

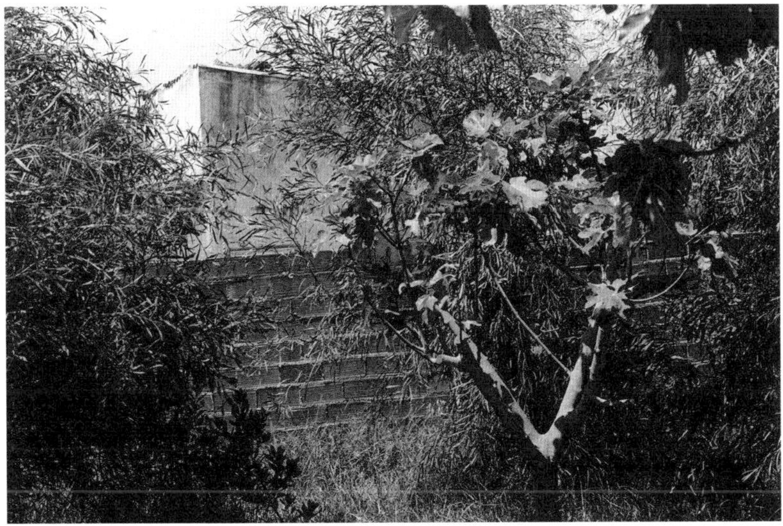

Figure 11.
Jean-Marc Bustamante.
From the series *Something
is Missing*, 1997 - present.

declare the bodily presence of the photographer within a sensory field and
to anchor a reading of the image in terms of an utterance designated by a first
person pronoun, or, to use Bertrand Russell's more apt and telling phrase,
by an 'egocentric particular', of which the word 'I' is the most prevalent form.
Thus these forms of photographic practice, in their casual prolificness, do
not so much represent the world as declare it to exist.

These types of practice, which are premised upon a presumption that
the photographer is the origin of that declaration, can be contrasted with
the very different kind of work produced by such photographers as Thomas
Struth, Candida Hoffer and Thomas Ruff in which scrupulously neutralised
forms of objectivity are striven for. Here the centre of operations is located
firmly in the apparatus itself rather than in the photographer. It is the camera
that points to the world and that operates as the deictic agent; it is the camera
that intervenes performatively to claim the event. Yet if anything yokes these
two apparently divergent types of practice together it is the way in which the
prioritisation of the deictic performativity of the photograph begins to undermine conventional notions of meaning and reference.

Geoff Bennington, in an exploration of the concept of the index and its
relationship to deixis, has pointed out the way in which the deictic sign stands
outside the referential space of language.[9] Where we can identify the meaning
of most words by consulting a dictionary definition, or examine, structurally,
the differential value of a word in its relationship to other words, deictics can

9 Geoff Bennington, 'Index',
in *Legislations: The Politics of
Deconstruction*, Verso,
London, 1994.

only be described grammatically in terms of their function and sphere of operations. The deictic term is always outside language, potentially subverting it and putting it into brackets; just as the performative hijacks the constative and reveals it to be provisional and contingent. The recognition of this gives new force to Barthes' prevailing intuition that the photograph ultimately preoccupies us because it lacks meaning, because, as Banfield, writing about Barthes, succinctly puts it: '...what the photograph is sensible of can be outside the ego, a thought unthought, unintended, involuntary and without meaning.'[10]

The work of the French artist Jean-Marc Bustamante exemplifies the problems that this raises for photography. Since the late 1990s he has produced a series of photographs called *Something is Missing*: images taken in a range of different cities such as Buenos Aires, Barcelona, Madrid, and Miami (Figure 11). The images at one level trace the familiar characteristics of non-places in the city, the arbitrary conjunctions and contingent events that conspire to construct the illegibility of the contemporary urban milieu. At one level these photographs are unremarkable, characterised by a flat banality that resists any offer of aesthetic engagement or narrative. Yet at another level it is that very emptiness that must preoccupy us, that very sense that something, indeed, is missing. There is, in these photographs, a sense of indeterminacy around the framing of the image, a sense that this frame is not so much a delimitation of a semiotic space, but more an arbitrary event, a performance, a gesture that points to the scene and in doing so points to our inability to read it. Like Barry's *Inert Gas Series* Bustamante's photographs, situated on the threshold between referentiality and legibility, point to the real while reminding us that photography can never represent it.

Photography in an Expanding Field:
Distributive Unity and Dominant Form
Peter Osborne

This essay is concerned with the ontology of photographic imagery. More specifically, it is concerned with the historical ontology of photographic imagery or the historically changing modes of being of the 'photographic'. As a matter of philosophical principle I take all ontology to be historical ontology, but some things are more historical – more radically subject to the temporality of the human – than others.[1] Photography is a practice that is currently undergoing profound and rapid historical changes, as a result of both technological and cultural-economic determinations. Technologically, digitally-produced imagery appears to sever that ontological tie between the photograph and its referent that hitherto defined the photographic as a distinct ontological form. In the sphere of cultural economy, the image-space of the photographic has expanded to global dimensions as a constituent part of what we might call photo-capitalism. If print-capitalism was a cultural-economic condition of nationalism,[2] photo-capitalism is a distinctively transnational (and translinguistic) cultural-economic form. As Régis Debray has argued: 'if you want to make yourself known everywhere and establish dominion over the world, manufacture images instead of writing books [...] this is the moral of the story which all empires have known, from the Byzantine to the American.'[3] The photographic image is, among other things, the dominant visual form of the American empire. As such, the analysis of current changes in the ontology of the photographic image promises to provide insight into both the historical ontology and the politics of cultural forms. This essay aims to contribute to the development of a theoretical framework for understanding these changes through reflection upon the conceptual form and ontological mode of 'the photographic'.

Understood historically, the question of the ontology of the photographic image is in large part the question of the mode of unity of the relational totality of the variety of different photographic forms coexisting within the present: chemical photography, film, television, video and digital imaging – to name only the five main forms, the spine, if you like, of a still expanding field. (One might also include the remote sensing of micro-wave, infra-red, ultra-violet, and short-wave radio imagery, for example.) This totality is relational,

1 That is to say, I don't accept the conceptual restrictions imposed by either the classical metaphysical, substance-based usage of 'ontology' or the early Heideggerian use of the term, which would distinguish in principle between Being *(Sein)* as the object of a 'fundamental' ontology and the merely 'ontic' status of beings or entities *(Seiendes)*. Rather, I use the term 'ontology' in a general sense to refer to any discourse about forms and modes of being. As such, ontology is an ineliminable aspect of philosophical discourse, however, critical, dialectical, historical or 'contextual' that discourse purports to be. Ontological agnosticism or indifference to ontology is, in this respect, the founding flaw of most semiotic theories of culture (C.S. Pierce's metaphysical and semiotic pragmatism excepted) and all Saussurean or exclusively code-based semiotics of the photograph, in particular. For an extended account of this distinction, as manifest in two different traditions of photographic theory, see my 'Sign and Image' in Peter Osborne, *Philosophy in Cultural Theory*, Routledge, London and New York, 2000, pp. 20–52.

2 See Benedict Anderson, *Imagined Communities: Reflections on the Origin and Spread of Nationalism*, Verso, London and New York, 1983, chapters 2 & 3.

3 Régis Debray, *Media Manifestos: On the Technological Transmission of Cultural Forms*, trans. Eric Rauth, Verso, London and New York, 1996, p.155.

4 Ibid., pp.141-2 – emphases added. One might reasonably be sceptical of Debray's claim that television lacks the 'reality effect' possessed by film; especially when, in his discussion of digital remixing, he describes the ontological 'inversion' involved in terms of the replacement of the criterion of 'anteriority' by that of 'actuality'. For what counts visually as 'actuality' here is thoroughly permeated by photographic norms themselves. One need only think of the role of faux-amateur techniques (all that hand-held camera) in contemporary televisual and filmic realism alike.

5 See Peter Osborne, *The Politics of Time: Modernity and Avant-Garde*, Verso, London and New York, 1995.

rather than expressive, because as a cultural-historical form there is no single underlying, ontologically fundamental basis to its unity – in a single technology, for example – which would allow for the specification of photography as a 'medium'. Indeed, in the sense in which it has been understood in the visual arts since Clement Greenberg, the question of medium-specificity is precisely the wrong question to ask of the photographic, since it is the peculiar generality of the photographic image – to which I will return – that laid the ground for the destruction of medium-specificity in the visual arts and the inauguration of what Rosalind Krauss calls the 'post-medium condition' (it is perhaps better called the 'transmedia' condition), as long ago as the end of the first decade of the twentieth century. The question of the unity of the photographic must thus be separated from the question of medium, at least in its Greenbergian sense. Greenbergian modernism generates an essentialist anxiety about medium-specificity that is unhelpful and misplaced. Rather, I shall suggest, the question of the unity of the photographic is the question of the ongoing socio-historical process of unification of the photographic as a cultural form. There is a technological basis to this unification – a particular history of technological relations – but it is their meanings-in-use that determine the (necessarily 'cultural') unity of these technologies.

It may be, as Debray insists, that the ontology of images must be 'answerable' to productive techniques, in as much as 'one simply does not take the same kind of photograph using a photographic plate exposed for two hours during the subject's tedious pose and using a Polaroid camera'. Yet Debray does not dispute (though he does not explain why) that both are photographs. It is equally true that:

> ...*The image when formed on a screen by the projection of light behind a photographic frame of film across a darkened room belongs to a* different order of 'signs' *from the image electronically induced by a cathodic current on a luminiferous surface.*

However, it is not clear that the television image does not, in itself, remain photographic, despite this electronic mediation (indeed, by virtue of the character of this electronic mediation).[4]

All such unities, being historical, are at once both retrospectively and prospectively constructed (in the sense of depending upon certain projections of the future, as well as certain receptions of the past), but they are nonetheless 'ontological' for that, since, as cultural forms, they partake of the complex historical temporality of existential ontology (in their being-for the human), writ large, at the level of social form. Cultural forms articulate specific modes of 'temporalization of history'.[5] And photography, perhaps, more intimately than most. One need look no further than the familiar literature on the existential charge of the photograph in its relationship not only to remembrance, but more fundamentally to death: Bazin's 'embalming' of time; the late Barthes's 'excessive, monstrous mode' of the 'immobilization' of time and hence 'sign of my future death'; even Bourdieu's function of 'solemnization'.[6] However, the relationship between the photographic preservation of the past, on the one hand, and historical experience more strictly speaking (and hence politics), on the other, is more theoretically complex and politically contested than this particular French tradition suggests, as earlier and more critical interpretations of the existential ontology of photographic imagery – in the writings of Kracauer and Benjamin – attest.[7]

The idea of the photographic, then, posits a certain cultural-historical unity to a particular set of technologies of image production. It groups together technically produced indexical images of various sorts, supplemented, more recently, by digital images in which such indexical effects are simulated in various ways. This unity derives from connections at the level of both the material form of the technologies (an imprinting of light upon light-sensitive surfaces of different kinds) and their predominant socio-cultural functions and uses (as epistemically privileged representations of the real). All technologies are by definition unstable unities of material form and social use: abstractions of the rationality (logos) of specific processes of making (techné) in the service of the generalization of their uses – as one can see in the very grammar of the term 'technology'. However, it is meaning – ontologically, one might say, 'structures of recognition' – that mediates, or constitutes the unity of, material form and social use: hence the characterization of technology as itself a cultural form, and the necessity for an ontologically-based semiotics, or metaphysically-grounded existential pragmatics, as the theoretical basis of its comprehension. Insofar as there is an adequate concept of the photographic, unifying its various instances, it will be a recovery at the level of theory of an implicit practical unity of forms of signification produced by a discrete set of combinations of material forms and their social uses. Technologies relate to one another on both of these axes.

There is thus no single thread in the history of a technological form like photography. This is the theoretical difficulty posed by its cultural character. So, to return to my initial question: what is the *conceptual form* and *ontological mode* of such a unity – the unity of 'the photographic' as a practical unity of forms of signification produced by a historically discrete set of combinations of material forms and social uses? I shall approach this question in two ways: first, philosophically, through a reworking of Kant's notion of distributive unity; second, cultural-historically, through the idea of 'the' photograph as an imagistic register of temporal singularity, which is taken as a metonym

6 André Bazin, 'The Ontology of the Photographic Image' (1945), in his *What is Cinema?* Volume One, trans. Hugh Gray, University of California Press, Berkeley, 1967, p.14; Roland Barthes, *Camera Lucida: Reflections on Photography* (1980), trans. Richard Howard, Fontana, London, 1984, pp.91, 96; Pierre Bourdieu et al, *Photography: A Middle-brow Art* (1965), trans. Shaun Whiteside, Stanford University Press, Standford, 1990, chapter 1.

7 See *Philosophy in Cultural Theory*, pp. 35ff.

or model that provides an imaginary ground for the unity of the photographic field. I will conclude, very briefly, by gesturing towards the central role in the historical articulation of the unity of this field played by dominant forms.

The unity of the photographic, I would suggest, is 'distributive' in form. As such it is implicated, interpretatively, in each individual photographic form. It is also present, more explicitly, in that social distribution of individual images across different material forms – beyond their ostensible boundaries as 'works' – that results from the reproducibility inherent in the photographic. The question of the ontological significance of the latest technological forms is thus less that of their materiality, in itself, than that of their effects upon the expanding field of the photographic as a whole. Hence my title: photography in an expanding (rather than an expanded) field. The expansion here is internally technologically generated, continuing and open-ended, rather than reducible to a discrete set of external relations.[8]

Distributive unity

The notion of distributive unity, as a logically distinct form of unity, derives from Kant's *Critique of Pure Reason*. Kant, however, thinks it there only negatively, as a threat to what he calls the 'collective' unity established by ideas, which, he argues, unites the actions of the understanding in its relations to intuitions and thereby makes a coherent experience of the world possible, over time, at the level of the whole. In Kant's terms (from the 'Appendix to the Transcendental Dialectic'):

> *Just as the understanding unites the manifold into an object through concepts, so reason on its side unites the manifold of concepts through ideas by positing a certain* collective unity *as the goal of the understanding's actions, which are* otherwise *concerned only with* distributive unity.[9]

In other words, without 'ideas' (in Kant's particular sense of concepts that posit objects beyond possible experience) there would be a merely 'distributive' unity to the acts of the understanding. The justification of the presumption of collective unity increasingly preoccupied Kant in the aftermath of the *Critique of Pure Reason*, since the need to assert the unity of nature as a teleological system, which collective unity involves, threatened to collapse his critical project back into a form of ontological rationalism. It is the alternative danger, however, that is relevant here: the threat of distributive unity as a breakdown of the conceptual unity of experience itself. For, as Kant put it in the 'First Introduction' to the *Critique of Judgement:*

> *... although experience forms a system in terms of* transcendental *laws, which comprise the conditions under which experience as such is possible, yet* **empirical** *laws might be so infinitely diverse, and the forms of nature*

8 My point of contrast here is Rosalind Krauss, 'Sculpture in the Expanded Field' (1979), in her *The Originality of the Avant-garde and Other Modernist Myths*, MIT Press, Cambridge MA and London, 1985, pp. 277-90 – in which it is a semiotically determinate transformation in the relations of sculpture to landscape and architecture that expands the field.

9 Immanuel Kant, *Critique of Pure Reason* (1781; 1787), trans. Paul Guyer and Allan Wood, Cambridge University Press, Cambridge, 1997, A644/B672 – emphasis added.

which pertain to particular experience so very heterogeneous, *that the concept of a system in terms of these (empirical) laws must be quite alien to the understanding, and... the possibility – let alone the necessity – of such a whole is beyond our grasp. And yet for particular experience to cohere thoroughly in terms of fixed principles, it **must** have this systematic coherence of empirical laws as well.*[10]

The threat of a merely distributive unity is the threat of a *heterogeneity to the forms of nature* beyond the 'logic of specification' (genus/species/subspecies) and hence of an *infinite diversity* of empirical laws. It is thus the paradox of Kant's conception of distributive unity that it is *not really a unity* at all at the level of the objects of 'experience', but rather denotes a type of oneness made up of the spatial contiguity and temporal continuity of experience alone. There is no unity to its objects. To put it another way: distributive unity is *aesthetic*, in the primary sense of the term, meaning 'of sensibility'. For Kant, distributive unity is thus, epistemologically, a *negative* construction or limit concept, produced by intellectually abstracting (in the sense of removing) from the empirical content of experience the subjectively necessary presupposition of the 'collective unity' imposed by ideas. If this collective unity cannot be plausibly constructed (and as I have said, Kant himself was progressively pushed back towards rationalist teleology in order to do it) the logic of distribution tends instead to the multiplication of singularities. This is the sense in which philosophies of difference are inherently aesthetic. It is, of course, Deleuze who draws this conclusion, and to whom we owe the extraction of the concept of distribution from Kant's work.[11] In the second chapter of *Difference and Repetition*, Deleuze takes Kant's negative conception of distributive unity and turns it into a positive ontological concept of distributive difference. This is, in many ways, the key concept of Deleuze's philosophy of difference: distributive difference within a univocity of being. This is Deleuze's ontology, in a nutshell.[12]

However, if there are to be subjects and objects of knowledge and experience, in whatever secondary or derived form, a 'belonging together' or what Kant called an 'affinity' of multiple singularities, must nonetheless occur – and hence be amenable to theoretical construction – in some form. As Deleuze and Guattari put it in *What is Philosophy?*: 'The problem of philosophy is how to acquire a consistency without losing the infinite into which thought plunges.'[13] Despite a certain Deleuzianism, then, the rhetoric of 'multiple singularities' cannot do away with the philosophical requirement of a construction of unity in or across distribution, at various levels of analysis, in order to render intelligible intelligibility itself. Hence the necessity for the development of Kant's concept of distributive unity beyond both Deleuze's ontological radicalization of distribution into 'difference in itself' and the

10 Immanuel Kant, *Critique of Judgement*, trans. Werner S. Pluhar, Hackett, Indianapolis/Cambridge, 1987, p. 392 - bold added.

11 The editors of the new Cambridge edition of Kant's *Works* don't consider the term 'distribution' significant enough to index.

12 Gilles Deleuze, *Difference and Repetition* (1968), trans. Paul Patton, Athlone Press, London, 1994.

13 Gilles Deleuze and Félix Guattari, *What is Philosophy?*, trans. Graham Burchell and Hugh Tomlinson, Verso, London and New York, 1994, p. 42.

14 Cf. Christian Kerslake,
'The Vertigo of Philosophy:
Deleuze and the Problem of
Immanence', *Radical Philosophy*
113 (May/June 2002), pp. 10-23.
Kerslake emphasizes the
constructive character of
Deleuze's concept of difference.
My suggestion here is that such
a construction will, of necessity,
yield a concept of absolute
difference with a greater
distributive unity than Deleuze
envisaged. It is the desire to
avoid this link between
construction and unity that
motivates the opposing, purely
affirmative reading of Deleuze's
'difference' recently defended
by Peter Hallward. See the
exchange between Christian
Kerslake and Peter Hallward,
'Justification or Affirmation?'
in *Radical Philosophy* 114
(July/August 2002), pp. 29-33.
The antinomical character of
this opposition is the result of
their mutual abstraction from
the problem of history.

logical restrictions of Kant's thought – which can think unity only as concept-lessness, subsumption or regulation – from which the 'radicalism' of Deleuze's solution itself ultimately derives.[14] Such a concept of distributive unity, I want to suggest, would articulate the *logical form of the historical unity of empirical forms* – a way of grasping the insecurely bounded, because constantly shifting, relational totalities of historical forms. The unity of the photographic is a distributive unity in this sense.

The photographic is distributed across a determinate, historically progressive range of technologico-cultural forms – the 'expanding field' – from early chemical photography, through negative-based prints, film, television and video to digital imaging. This unity is not conceptual in the *Kantian* sense. Rather, I would suggest, it derives from a chain of relations between technologies that is sustained as a distributive unity by their common cultural functions. In this sense, a distributive unity is a pragmatic unity. It is a condition of this commonality of function that the types of images produced share a certain *de*-materialized generality that transcends their technologically particular material forms and acts as a kind of relay between them. It is important, however, to resist the temptation of conceiving of this de-materialized generality as some kind of shared 'essence', since it is ontologically dependent in each instance on a specific technological basis – hence the distributive rather than collective unity of the photographic image-space. Nonetheless, as the founding site of the technological determination of an image, the ontological meaning of which transcends its material form, 'the photograph' (or, more specifically, the still photographic image) has served historically as a kind of metonymic model for the photographic as a whole. It is this metonymic modelling that is thrown into crisis by the potential for 'ontological inversion' inherent in digital technologies: that is, non-indexical photographs. However – and this is my point – this crisis in a particular *imagined* unity is not necessarily a crisis (although it does correspond to a transformation) in the *actual* distributive unity of the field.

The photograph: metonymic model for an imagined unity of the field
The idea of a founding unity of the photographic (like other ideas of founding unities) is essentially imaginary or mythical: in this case, in its reductive identification of a cultural form with a technology – the ideological fantasy of a 'medium', in Greenberg's sense. Yet it is the social actuality of this mythological identification (its social being *qua* structure of recognition, as inscribed in the social practices of photography) that give social reality to photography as a cultural form. There is a constitutive illusion here. Photography, in other

words, from this point of view, is a cultural category the unity of which is based on the imagined and practiced unification of a particular technological process (optical/mechanical/chemical) and a particular set of social functions (the solemnization of festivity/documentation/pornography/ advertising/ surveillance etc). This imagined unity is condensed into the famous *meaning-effect of 'the real'*. This is at once a naturalization of the structure of the theological image – signification via participation in the real, or what Bazin called the object-image (for photography is without doubt a theological technology) – and an aesthetically novel form of indexical signification, rooted in the technological specificity of the photographic process: that combination of seamless material continuity and tonal differentiation characteristic of its alleged 'analogical perfection'.[15] The identification of the process (photography) with a particular quality of experience (the photographic image) is summed up in the ideal objecthood of the photograph. Yet it is here, on closer inspection, in the very idea of 'the photograph', that this ontological unity is least secure (or, better, most ideal), since it too is actually distributed, both spatially and temporally, across of a number of discrete sites.

15 Cf. *Philosophy in Cultural Theory*, pp. 29-41.

The disarmingly simple question of *where* 'the photograph' is, is famously difficult to answer. Is it, for example, as ordinary language suggests, to be identified with the photographic print? Hardly, for this is (at least potentially) a multiple – although a print is one place it might be found. Is it the negative? But this is a negative or tonally inverted image (and anyway a film might remain undeveloped). Is it, then, the image captured on the photographic plate or film? After all, photographs are what one 'takes' – one each instance, however many prints. Yet this is, perversely, unviewable, until developed. It soon becomes clear that to ask 'where is the photograph?' is the wrong question. Put simply there is no single site of the photograph. The photograph is not the kind of thing, ontologically, that can be strictly identified in spatial terms. There is a distributive unity to 'the' photograph itself, as well as to the broader field of the photographic. Insofar as the question can be meaningfully addressed, the photograph is distributed *across* the sites of its process, which it permeates as an image, de-realized (spectral), albeit in a peculiar ontological state of dependency upon the processes that it transcends, in each of its different technological forms: hence its peculiar combination of generality and specificity. There is an ontological affinity here between photography and conceptual art, or, more generally, the conceptual aspect of all art. For there is no fixed place for either the photograph or the work of art.

The photograph, then, like the work of art, is an ideal unity. It is held together by the idea of the 'capture' of a moment of time; an idea which is given cultural actuality by the dependence of its social functions upon the meaning-effect of the 'real'. Yet this supposedly fixed temporal singularity is phantasmatic, since the temporality of the photographic image is always that of a relation between a (constantly shifting) 'now' and the photograph's 'then' – a relation sustained, *as if* atemporal, by the material continuity of the photographic form in question. It is the spatial boundedness of the image that secures the illusion of temporal objectivity – the idea that time itself might become an 'object'. A photograph is an *objective illusion* of temporal objectification. Subsequent photographic forms – film, television, video, digital – derive their meaning from their historical relations to this primary form: in particular, from the appropriation and technological extension of both its idea and its cultural functions.

Dominant form

Historically, it would seem that the most technologically advanced cultural form, in each instance, becomes the dominant form: that form in relation to which other cultural forms derive their historical meaning, and to which they progressively 'adapt' themselves in various ways.[16] It also seems that, to begin with, each new form models itself on aspects of the previous dominant form that it will replace before the relationship becomes inverted: photography modelled itself on painting, film on photography, television on film, video on film and television, digital on video, etc. In Althusserian terms, one might thus say that, historically, distributive unity is 'structured in dominance' by dominant forms.[17] The current 'crisis' in the concept of the photographic – such as it is – marks the transition to a new dominant form. The question of the impact on the concept of the photographic of the 'ontological inversion' represented by digital re-mixing (with its ironic return to painterly modes of composition) is thus the question of what sets of relations will be established, in practice, between the new and the old forms. Despite its ontological character, there will be no answer to this question in advance of practical developments – no theoretical pre-determination – if, as I have argued, the ontological issue is that of the historical character of the distributive unity of the totality of forms.

16 The most technologically advanced cultural form also means the form most productive for new cultural functions – since technological 'advance' is always relative to cultural function as much as it is to strictly scientific achievement.

17 See Louis Althusser, 'Contradiction and Overdetermination: Notes for an Investigation', in his *For Marx* (1966), trans. Ben Brewster, New Left Books, London, 1977, pp. 87-128. This is particularly clear in the case of painting, which has had to adapt itself successively to photography, film, television and video – a history that is itself thematised in the shifting uses of abstraction by a post-conceptual painter like Richter. See my 'Images abstraites: Signe, image et esthétique dans la peinture de Gerhard Richter', *La Part de l'Oeil*, nos 17-18, 2001/2, pp. 229-39.

Thinking Things
Olivier Richon

Where is the photograph?

The question 'Where is the photograph?' presupposes that we have lost sight
of photography or that photography is somehow lost; that it has lost a direction
perhaps or that we do not find it where it should be; that it has been misplaced;
that it remains somewhere, unclaimed, in some lost property office of culture.

One could answer that photography as such is less solid; it hasn't
been liquidated, of course, but it is more liquid; it has dissolved into *the
photographic*. What is this? Craig Owens remarked that 'the discourse of the
art world was identified with *the photographic*'. By this he meant 'the notion
of the photographic as opposed to photography per se, theorisation of the
photographic in terms of its multiples copies: no reflection of originality in
the original, timed with "the death of the author", the mechanisation of image
production'.[1] The photographic is a programmatic term that entails a position
calling into question the status of origins and originality in terms of what is
pictured and who pictures it. Such a programme arises from the shift from a
noun, *photography* to an adjective *photographic*, which in turn takes the place
and value of a noun: *the photographic*. Now, as we know, grammar is never
innocent. If the adjective 'photographic' means *of* or *relating to* photography,
exactly what does it relate or refer to? Linguistics tells us that adjectives, unlike
nouns, precisely have a problem with reference; an adjective hasn't got the
power to constitute objects. It can participate in the description of an object
but such description can only produce reference if there is a noun. Thus what
interests Bazin, for instance, isn't an ontology of photography but of the
photographic image.

Yet by making a noun out of an adjective, the notion of 'the photographic'
registers a sense of loss for a fixed referent. If, therefore, the photographic

1 Craig Owens, *Beyond
Recognition*, University of
California Press, 1992, p.300

suggests an activity and a process rather than a specific medium or discipline that moves *beyond photography* as such, it is also linked to a certain ontology, as it attempts to address the question of *'what is photography?'*. Craig Owens answered this question by promoting the authorless aspect of the medium and the medium's relation to questions of origin and originality. Starting from Roland Barthes' critique of conventional literary criticism, where the life and intentions of the author explains the work, Owens evokes 'the death of the author' as a parricide necessary for the birth of the reader, or reading as a critical practice. The suggestion here, perhaps, is that the photographic isn't really about photography but about a certain literary or textual attitude towards the photograph, the attitude of a reader of signs. This privileging of the textual as a form of inscription isn't really surprising if we recall that historically a critical reflection upon the photographic image owes much to literature and cinema (Antonioni, Baudelaire, Bazin, Barthes, Benjamin, Calvino, Kracauer, Metz, Mulvey, Sontag, Proust and others) and relatively less to art history and theory.[2]

Yet one might ask why Owens, in addressing the issue of the photographic, began by linking photography to the death of the author? Would it have been more appropriate to link it to the author's absence instead? This is what Bazin did when he wrote that 'the presence of man is the basis of all artistic activity; only in photography do we delight in its absence'.[3] There are no apologies for absence here. No sick note excusing the absence of someone but praise and an enjoyment of the empty space left by the author's departure. (Of course, Bazin's view has been cruelly yet hastily criticised from various points of view, from a constructionist theory of meaning to a modernist awareness of photography's rhetoric. Yet, perhaps, this is to miss the point).

Absence and automatism bring us to the last point of Owens' *photographic*: that of the mechanisation of image production. It is a well-known theme of Benjamin's artwork essay that the technical properties of the medium in themselves may change the status and function of art, of art as reproduction. Jacques Rancière, in *Le Partage du sensible* (Dividing the Senses) is suspicious – and, of course, he is not the first – of the critical force of mechanical arts as such.[4] He sees a problem in deducing the aesthetic and political properties of an art form by reference to its technical properties. For Rancière, the mechanical arts must first be practiced and recognised as arts and not merely as techniques of reproduction and diffusion. Technique is understood as serving a form of communication and is distinguished from a process of meaning. In terms of meaning, figures of the mechanical, the anonymous, the simple and the banal are first elevated to the dignity of subjects in painting (Courbet; Manet) and literature (Zola; Balzac; Flaubert) and are only later incorporated into

   Where is the Photograph? **Philosophies**

---

2 In connection with this relationship between photography and the cinema we should note that Barthes is also responsible for turning an adjective into a noun. In his essay 'The Third Meaning', a text primarily concerned with frozen frames from Eisenstein's *Ivan the Terrible*, Barthes proposes to call those details to be found in the stilled image that resist communication and signification, *the filmic*. The filmic is like a photograph, like a fragment or a fetish that freezes and subverts the diegesis of the film. It enables a vertical reading into the semiotics of arrested motion: details of faces, object, in short, an attention upon the make up of the image. The filmic is within a still image, a photographic fragment that opens up this 'third meaning', made up of signifiers which resist signification. See Roland Barthes, 'The Third Meaning, in *Image, Music, Text*, trans. S. Heath, Fontana, 1977, pp. 52-68. A similar subversion of the diegesis of the film is noted by Gianni Celati who compares the frontal view in the photographs of Walker Evans with that of the films of Antonioni: 'the frontal view amounts to a choice of a low threshold of intensity, of a narrative mode which avoids excitement and relates everything back to a calm, composed style of representation'. Thus the frontal view reintroduces waiting in our act of looking. One is not waiting for something to happen, as with narrative time; there is no action. Here, the reader of signs views the image in slow motion as it were, and the activity of looking and reading does not aim to kill time to relieve the anxiety associated with waiting for something to happen. In Seymour Chapman & Guido Fink, eds., *L'Avventura*, Rutgers University Press, 1989.

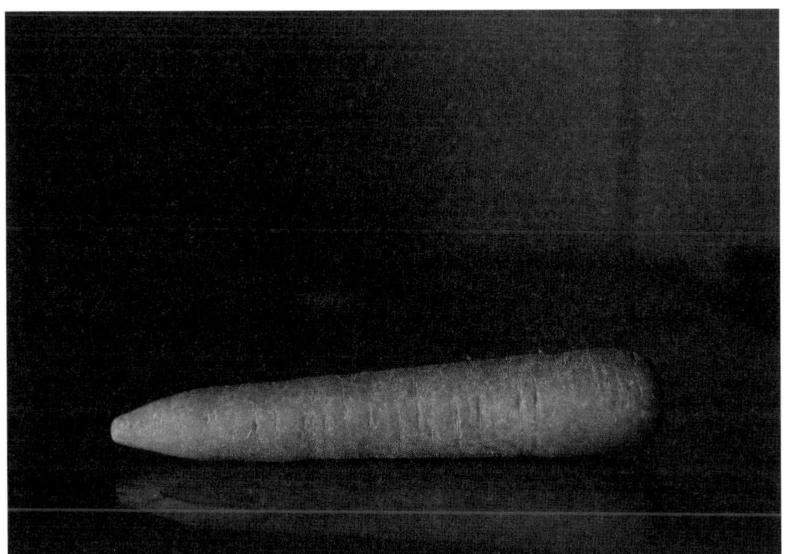

Figure 12. Olivier Richon,
A Real Allegory (with carrot),
2002.

photography and cinema. Thus Claude Lantier, the painter and hero of Zola's novel *The Masterpiece* (L'Oeuvre) can find in a vegetable a template for a revolution in painting:

> *Wasn't a bunch of carrots, yes, a bunch of carrots, studied directly and painted simply, personally, as you see it yourself, as good as any of the routine, cut and dried Ecole des Beaux-Arts stuff, painted with tobacco juice? The day was not far off when a solitary, original carrot might be pregnant with revolution.*[5]

The shift from multiplicity, a bunch of carrots, to uniqueness, a *single* carrot, transforms this vegetable – whose form after all isn't totally innocent – into an emblem for Realism. In the economy of signs, this solitary carrot 'pregnant with revolution' recalls that synecdoche and metonymy are the privileged tropes of literary realism. As synecdoche, a single, solitary carrot stands for all carrots. (Figure 12) This power to generalise is also the power of the didactic example that starts with the particular to aim for the general. This is achieved by zooming in and focusing on one object, an object 'studied directly' and 'as you see it yourself'. The emphasis is on details, fragments, and anecdotes as signs that construct a reality effect based upon an art of description. Thus the emphasis on metonymy: a concentration on details and a mode of observation that may reach clinical intensity. In *L'Effet de Réel*, Barthes calls attention to literary descriptions whose function appears to be unnecessary and superfluous to the general structure of the narrative.[6] This emphasis on descriptive details as a gratuitous supplement is a forerunner to

3 André Bazin, *L'Ontologie de l'image photographique*, Editions du Cerf, France, 1965. Unpublished translation by Luke Thurston

4 Jacques Rancière, *Le Partage du Sensible*, La Fabrique Editions, Paris, 2000, pp. 46 - 53. I am grateful to Mauricio Guillen for introducing me to this text.

5 Emile Zola, *The Masterpiece*, Elek Books, Great Britain, 1950, p. 45.

6 Roland Barthes, *The Rustle of Language*, Basil Blackwell, Oxford, 1986.

the 'third meaning' that Barthes finds within the film still. When descriptions do not serve action and communication, they may serve to embellish the narrative and are endowed with an aesthetic value. Yet when the narrative presents itself as the narration of history, descriptive details provide a varnish of authenticity to the narrative of history. Thus it is not a coincidence that literary realism is contemporary with the writing of history understood as an accumulation of facts, and photography understood as a way of recording things: each privileges an idea of the real as a concrete and self sufficient entity which exists independently of its representation. It is as if the real is passively waiting to be described by the historian or recorded by the photographer. Yet is a photograph like a description, or do photographs just show things? Are they a visual equivalent of a description that supplants the role of language, a sort of automatic depiction based on the model of these descriptions that guarantees the reality-effect of a text?

Discussion of the photograph as an index of the real is a more recent way of accounting for its reality effect. Bazin writes about the photographic image as an imprint or a Veronica Shroud in a way that suggests an understanding of the photograph as an index of the real. Yet Bazin always privileges the object to the detriment of the sign. As Peter Wollen has written: 'Bazin repeatedly stresses the existential bond between sign and object, which for Peirce was the determining characteristic of the indexical sign. But whereas Peirce made his observation in order to found a logic, Bazin wishes to found an aesthetic'.[7] Rancière is equally suspicious of generalising the indexical as the essence of the photograph but for a different reason, as he sees this move as belonging to the postmodern discourse on the photograph and not to photography as a historically constituted practice. For Rancière, aesthetic changes precede technical changes. The glory of the banal and the everyday only belongs later to photography, as with the canonical works of Atget, Evans and Sander. The ordinary is thus an aesthetic category based upon the repudiation of the classical regime of representation that assigns a hierarchy to different genres and subjects. The banal and the ordinary raise things to the dignity of objects and the technique of photography enables us to read signs on the photographed body of things and people. Yet for Rancière, the ordinary requires some opacity to avoid being just that: an empirical and positivist fact to be transmitted or communicated. It needs to be read as a hieroglyph, as a mythological and phantasmagoric figure. For Rancière the fascination with the ordinary and the banal resides in the way in which art and literature can make us aware of the opacity of the object. For him, this project is similar to that of Marx's elaboration of commodity fetishism, where the banality of commodities is given a phantasmagorical dimension. Thus Marx's famous example of a table

7 Peter Wollen, *Signs and Meanings in the Cinema*, Secker & Warburg, London, 1969, p. 126.

in the 'Fetishism of the commodity and its secret'. When wood is turned into a table, the table continues to be wood but 'as soon as it emerges as a commodity, it changes into a thing which transcends sensuousness ... it not only stands with its feet on the ground, but in relation to all other commodities, it stands on its head, and evolves out of its wooden brain grotesque ideas.'[8] The term 'grotesque' brings to mind the darkness of a grotto, and the darkness of the camera obscura, another site for reversals, where things in the world stand on their heads and form an upside down image, an image which occludes and yet maintains our relation to things.

8 Karl Marx, *Capital*, vol 1, Penguin Books, Harmondsworth, 1976, p.163.

The object

For a long time the word 'object' hasn't had a good press. We might recall that Susan Sontag once stated that 'to photograph people is to violate them, by seeing them as they never see themselves, by having knowledge of them they can never have; it turns people into objects that can be symbolically possessed'.[9] However, in this iconoclastic warning, the opposition between an observing subject and a represented object runs a bit too smoothly. It not only presupposes a given subject and an observable object; it also prioritizes the former over the latter. Can we add some shadows to this subject/object opposition and render it less transparent?

9 Susan Sontag, *On Photography*, Penguin Books, Harmondsworth, 1978, p.14.

Jean Baudrillard, in his recent texts on photography, reverses the common sense priority of the subject over the object. He certainly knows something about objects. We can recall his *System of Objects*, about the consumption of signs, which was published in 1968, a few years after Georges Perec's novel *Things*. For Baudrillard, it is the photographed object, the object as image that places us as subjects. To some extent, the object as image is a Bazinian theme. Commenting on Surrealism's use of the photographic image of the everyday Bazin writes that: 'Every image has to be experienced as an object, and every object as an image'.[10] Yet, for Bazin, photography carries with it a baroque impulse: stillness and *trompe l'oeil* achieve 'the complete satisfaction of our appetite for illusion through a mechanical reproduction which excludes man'. The oral dimension of our gaze is evidenced in this 'appetite for illusions'. Baudrillard, on the other hand, is more concerned with the appetite of the object for the spectator. The object consumes us and 'It is the object which thinks us', he writes. 'We can only see the object if it looks at us ... Such is the hope or secret demand: to be seen, desired and thought about by the object and the world'.[11] It isn't me who takes a picture, rather it is the picture which takes me. As the psychoanalyst Darian Leader puts it, 'far from being picture capturing devices, humans are perpetually being caught by pictures. An image or picture is a human capturing device'.[12] The gaze of the object has a priority

10 A. Bazin, op. cit

11 Jean Baudrillard, 'C'est l'objet qui nous pense', in *Fotographies/Photographies/ Photographs 1985–1998*, P. Weibel, ed, Cantz, Germany 1999. The translation is my own.

12 Darian Leader, *Stealing the Mona Lisa: what art stops us from seeing*, Faber and Faber, London 2002, p.25.

13 ibid, p. 17

14 Slavoj Zizek, *Looking Awry*, MIT Press, Cambridge, Mass. and London, 1991, p.118.

over our gaze. This is, of course, also a Lacanian idea: that before looking we are being looked at, that our gaze is dependent upon somebody else's gaze. To complicate the canonical art school assumption – once popularized by John Berger – that 'seeing comes before words', we might say instead that being seen comes before seeing. That there is a split between seeing and being seen is evident in the unease produced by these portraits with eyes appearing to follow us: 'the fact that a portrait can instill unease in this way is another example of how we often feel looked at by something that does not see us'.[13] In the same way, Slavoj Zizek has remarked that the notorious house in Hitchcock's *Psycho* looks back: 'Lilah sees the house, but nonetheless she cannot see it at the point from which it gazes back at her'.[14] Something that does not see may have a more unsettling effect, like the eyes of the blind, the glass eyes of stuffed animals or the dead eyes of fish. For Lacan, it is a point of light that turns us into pictures, recalling Freud's fetishist who is turned on by a shine on the nose. Light turns me into a photographic image: 'hence it comes about that the gaze is the instrument through which light is embodied and through which – if you will allow me to use a word, as I often do, in a fragmented form – I am photo-graphed'.[15]

15 Jacques Lacan, *The Four Fundamental Concepts of Psychoanalysis*, Penguin Books, Harmondsworth, 1979, p.106.

Baudrillard emphasizes objects as embodying this gaze which looks at us yet does not see us. The gaze of the object is responsible for the eclipse of the subject: 'the object is still for a certain time the vivid site of the disappearance of the subject'. Normally in photography it is the disappearance of the object that is commented upon but 'the subject also disappears on the other side of the lens. Every click of the shutter puts an end to the presence of the object and also causes my disappearance as subject'.

In Baudrillard's *Car l'illusion ne s'oppose pas à la réalité* we read that:
...you think you photograph such a scene for your enjoyment, in fact it is the scene which wishes to be photographed ... The subject is only the agent for the ironic appearance of things ... To photograph is not to consider the world as object, it is to turn the world into an object.[16]

16 Jean Baudrillard, Car l'illusion ne s'oppose pas à la réalité, Descartes & Cie, Paris, 1998. The translations are my own.

Why this praise of the object? Because the object does not pose, it has not been through a 'mirror stage'. Objects have no imaginary identification with themselves: 'having no problem of resemblance, they are marvelously identical to themselves'. The subject, the photographer, on the other hand, becomes an object in the photographic act: 'the object must be fixed, looked at intensely and frozen by the gaze. It is not the object which must pose it is he, the photographer, who must hold one's breath to create a void in time and in the body'. For Baudrillard, 'the magic of photography is that it is the object which does all the work', just as for Bazin, it is the mechanical recording and absence of subjectivity which produces what he calls a hallucination, a confusion between image and object.

Portraits

Baudrillard dreams of a photographic practice which is not concerned with messages, which has nothing to do with reportage or art. A sort of private practice beyond meaning and communication, a radical amateurism which privileges the taking of the photograph, the photographic act, and somehow almost loses interest in the image as such. (Obviously there is an element of provocation in this position as his own photographs have been exhibited, published, celebrated, and commented upon). If Baudrillard is celebrating an aesthetic of disappearance, he clearly is uneasy about one thing: portraits. And there are hardly any amongst his photographs. He finds it difficult to photograph people or faces, difficult – as he explains – to get to the mask hidden behind the identity of the face. Too much striving for identity in the portrait, there is no alterity as with animals. An animal has no identity psychologically speaking but has 'this charm of these beings which are alien to their image'.[17]

Yet is a portrait just a portrait? For the psychoanalyst Ferenczi, the most primary form of symbolism equates a part of the body with another, leading one part of the body to replace another. He notes the overemphasis of the upper part of the body in general, the lower half being repressed. Thus for Ferenczi, 'each part of the face becomes the representative of one or more genital areas'. 'I have no doubt', he writes, 'that the sense of embarrassment one experiences at being stared at, and which keeps one from staring hard at others, finds its explanation in the sexual- symbolic significance of the parts of the face'.[18] Could we now think of portraiture as an art of depicting displaced genitalia, as in Magritte's well-known painting *Le Viol* (1934). Godard is another also sensitive to such displacements. He notes that in *Vertigo*, there is an indication that Hitchcock films women's faces as if they were backsides, thus his preference for round and smooth faces and his avoidance (regretted by Godard) to exploit this feature with his male characters.[19] The truth of portraiture as a mirror of the soul, or as a reflection of the personality of the sitter, would be radically undermined by this return of what lies below and what lies behind. In this respect, Freud's case study of fetishism, locating the fetish in a shine on the nose that was produced by a glance at the nose, is another example of portraiture within which sexual symbolism is inscribed. It also recalls the vantage point from below of many socialist realist portraits whose phallic rigidity escapes no one.

What is meant here by 'symbol' needs commenting upon. Ernest Jones in his *Theory of Symbolism* of 1916, distinguishes between the psychoanalytic

17 The question of the portrait has haunted the history of photography. Whilst for Benjamin, the early portraits still contain an 'aura' and are part of the golden age of photography, portraiture as an artistic industry is at the core of Baudelaire's attack on the new medium. Baudelaire's rant is telling. It is against the narcissism of the rising bourgeoisie that is satisfied by photographic resemblance. It is the victory of narcissistic identity and the triumph of trite realism as the ideological function of art: photography guarantees the narcissism of photographed subjects and the narcissism of photographers proud of their faithful copy.

18 Sandor Ferenczi,' Symbolism', in *First Contributions to Psychoanalysis*, Karnak Books, London 1994, p.273.

19 Joan Luc Godard, *Cahiers du Cinéma*, 300, Editions de l'Etoile, Paris, 1979, p.12.

sexual symbol and the sexual symbolism found in folklore, myths, fairy
tales and jokes. The latter is cultural and the former is unconscious. On the
interpretation of the psychoanalytic symbol, Jones tells us that the individual
has no idea of what it means and that interpretation is met 'with surprise,
incredulity and repugnance'.[20] Yet symbolism generally is a form of thinking
with images, of making analogies, correspondences and identifications between
things. It is a more archaic form of mental activity, closer to the dreamwork,
and one could say, closer to image making. Thus, 'a tired man', says Jones,
'usually prefers looking at an illustrated newspaper, where ideas are presented
on a sensorial plane, to reading'. Despite the infinite material capable of
generating symbols, their meaning is basic and alarmingly repetitive: sex, love,
relatives, birth, and death. Jones's own contribution to the theory of symbolism
is his famous study of Punch and Judy, revealing Punch – this short, unruly,
funny little man – as an angry male organ. It sheds a new light on the symbolism
of dwarfs, gnomes and goblins, and transforms *Snow White and the Seven Dwarfs*
into an x-rated movie. Freud was weary of hastily assigning a pre-existing
meaning to a symbol outside of the dreamer's specific associations. Yet despite
this caution, he provides us with an exhaustive list that reads like a   collection
of trophies, of frozen images as clear and detached as a series of photographs:

> *emperor, empress: parents*
> *prince, princess: the dreamer*
> *rooms: women*
> *fish, snails, cat, mice and luggage: genitals*
> *open and locked doors; landscapes and hills: female genitals*
> *weapons and ties: male genitals*
> *steps, ladders, staircases: the sexual act*
> *baldness, hair-cutting, falling out of a tooth, decapitation: castration*
> *small animals and vermin: undesired brothers and sisters* [21]

As Darian Leader has argued, symbols may be more interesting than
the genitals they are supposed to represent. If early psychoanalysis seeks the
genital behind the symbol, a later view would stress that a symbol only hides
more symbols and that we will never get to the reality behind it.[22]

This is also true of the photographic: images are often more interesting
than the things they are supposed to represent. Images only hide more images
and we will never get to the reality behind them. If we do, it is at the risk of
encountering a bitter disappointment. This is what happens to the narrator
of the *Remembrance of Things Past*. Marcel, who had worshipped the photograph
of the great tragic actress Berma, is thoroughly disappointed the first time
he sees her on stage, as if reality could only shrink or deplete the image. In
Time Regained, it is the reality of ageing which transforms Berma into a kind

20 Ernest Jones, 'The Theory
of Symbolism', in *Papers on
Psychoanalysis*, Karnak, London,
1979, pp. 87 - 144

21 Sigmund Freud,
'Representation by Symbols',
in *The Interpretation of Dreams*,
Penguin Books,
Harmondsworth, 1976,
pp. 470 - 477.

22 Darian Leader, op. cit., p.80.

of sculptural object. Deserted by her friends, with death 'written all over her face', Berma has almost turned into a marble statue: 'The dying eyes were still relatively alive, by contrast at least with the terrible ossified mask, and glowed feebly like a snake asleep in the midst of a pile of stones'. It is thus not surprising that 'nothing now in her face recalled the countenance of which the photograph, one distant New Year's day had so disturbed me'.[23] The mineral rigidity of death perhaps offers a final image which, unlike the stillness of a photograph, this time does not refer to other images, yet which still conjures up other images, so that we will keep on looking.

23 Marcel Proust, *Time Regained*, Chatto & Windus, London, 1981, p.1049.

The Blind Train-spotter: A Delirium of Doubt
Pavel Büchler

The title of this essay is an accident of free association. It originates not in an interest in the nostalgic charms of transport fetishism but in a random reminder of quite another obsession, that of spotting 'current trends' in what we conventionally understand as 'contemporary' art.[1] While the former seems perfectly innocuous to me, I see the latter as a feature of a crisis of those conventions, and hence of the *function* of contemporary art, in a culture that, on the one hand, demands of artists that they provide a sense of contemporaneity, novelty and innovation, whilst on the other hand, it strives for an almost immediate obsolescence of their efforts as a hallmark of their (con)temporary relevance. And while railway enthusiasm certainly has much to tell about photography's demotic forms, I am more concerned with, and indeed worried about, what makes *us*, a handful of diligent 'trend-spotters' in the field of the visual arts, ask: 'Where is the photograph?' Why is it that from our vantage point we seem to have lost sight of it? The mode and the circumstances of the question beg further questions: Are we looking in the right place? If so, why can't we see it? Do we know what we are looking for? Perhaps not, since we are also asking: 'What is the photograph?' And, above all: Why do we need to keep asking such questions?

In short, posing the question of the photograph's whereabouts today, means that we believe that the status of this theoretical generalisation – that is, 'the photograph' – is somehow, strangely unstable or that our perspective has shifted, or both. Why? Faced with these questions, I will assume, provisionally, that while photographs are everywhere, *the* photograph, singular by definition, can only be in one place. It is probably not in contemporary art or not in the works of contemporary art, including those that 'use' photography, but it may be that contemporary art could show us where to look. Where is it then? And why are we *talking* about the photograph when what we really want to see is what has become of photography in this culture and what that has to say about where we are.

Herein may lie a clue. 'The photograph' is an abstraction. It is not *a* photograph, a generic approximation or a common denominator of all photographs.[2] Nor is it some elusive ingredient or an essence that makes

1 The train of my thought was set in motion by the news of a prominent contemporary arts organisation changing the guidelines for the appointment of artists to serve on the governing Board. While many members of the Board, representing an array of professional backgrounds, have been in position for a decade, it was decided that the tenure of artists should be limited to three years. The rational for this was that the organisation should be in touch with 'current trends in contemporary art'.

2 Interestingly, in generalising 'the photograph' most writers have purged the concept of one or another uses of photography – the banal snapshot, technical reproduction, forensic image, studio still-life.

many photographs 'worth looking at'. Rather it is a *manner of talking* about photography – a convention of theory that makes some but not all characteristics, traits, traditions and *problems* of photography worth talking about. Indeed, 'the photograph' may be our way of *problematising* photography, articulating its difficulty. In its guise as 'the photograph', photography has become problematical: curiously politicised, a suspect of many evils as well as their ambiguous witness, an instrument of awesome powers of manipulation as well as their victim, an accomplice of history as well as an estranged bystander, a big brother and a whipping boy. Whilst its technological foundations made photography seem once so full of promise, now they seem hardly relevant. Whilst its attentiveness to life and social action made it once seem aligned with progressive agendas of modernisation, now it seems hopelessly confusing. And whilst once photography was modern par excellence (and in some ways has stayed modern – which may be one of its problems), now photographs seem merely contemporary by default. So, what's happened?

*   *   *

The use of a pun in writing or speech is invariably apologetic: 'if I may...', 'forgive...'. Following in that time-honoured tradition of polite insincerity, I should concede at once that the title of this essay – whose genesis helped to prop up my semi-improvised oral presentation at the conference with an anecdote – bears the marks of mischievous recklessness. Or worse, it betrays a degree of prejudice. A speculation about such things as the conventions and terms that determine the critical reception of photography in and by contemporary art should examine more dispassionately how the 'contemporary' itself is determined. On reflection, however, this troublesome phrase reveals a certain metaphorical potential that warrants its survival here. This resides in a dialectic signalled by Walter Benjamin's well-known correction of Marx's allegory of revolutions as the locomotives of world history. In Benjamin's opinion, they are more like the applications of emergency brakes to runaway trains.

'The locomotive is *the* example of a utopian image of the power that man could attain with the machine.'[3] From Turner's *Rain, Steam and Speed* of 1844 and Berlioz's celebratory *Gesang der Eisenbahn* of 1846, through Monet's *Gare Saint-Lazare* three decades on, and a plethora of subsequent star appearances in poetry, visual arts or film (which reached something of a zenith of audience credibility with crowds of spectators reportedly fleeing early movie theatres to escape locomotives approaching from the screen), to the collision between a train engine and an automobile staged by Wolf Vostell as a happening in 1965,[4] the symbolism of the locomotive has travelled a long way. On its journey it had followed the tensions in critical thinking about the interdependency of

3 Roger Bahrens, 'Welcome to the Machine: The Instrument, the Technique, and the Utopia in Music', *Issues in Contemporary Culture and Aesthetics*, No. 2, October 1995, p.57.

4 Vostell's own methodological term, 'de-collage', hides another transport connection. It was derived from a French newspaper headline announcing a crash of an aeroplane immediately after décollage (the French for 'take-off').

technological promise and socio-cultural reality and, for my purposes in particular, about contemporary art as a mediating force between technical capability and its applications, and the sense of possibility and purpose in the self-conception of modern culture.

'The view from the train was not the view from the horse', declares Robert Hughes with an air of authority in *The Shock of the New*.[5] As the observation is hardly shocking in itself, he hastens to elaborate on how, at first, the 'succession and superimposition of views, the unfolding of landscape … compressed more motifs into the same time', while 'conversely, it left less time in which to dwell on any one thing'. This accelerated vision, at once expanded and compressed, brought about by the 'machine on wheels', was an aspect of a technological change 'so fast that it left art stranded'.[6] 'But', Hughes writes, 'because it promised to telescope more experience into the conventional frame of travel, and finally to burst the frame altogether, the avant-garde of engineering seemed to have something in common with the avant-garde of art'.

Being *absolument moderne*, as Rimbaud demanded, required the artistic avant-garde to proclaim faith in the liberating potential of the new space opened up by scientific discovery, technological innovation, enterprise and engineering genius, and in the capacity of art to understand and mediate 'the new' as an agent of change. To be modern meant to be *with* the 'machine', both to reflect the conditions of change and to idealise them, to identify the new in the contemporary as an index of value. By the time the arrival of the avant-garde proper was announced in the *Futurist Manifesto* on the front page of *Le Figaro* in 1909, art began to display machine-like features not (yet) in its performance but in the principles of organisation into 'movements' and the operating critical 'rules' that came with it. And, by the time the avant-garde signed off with the last issue of *Internationale Situationiste* sixty years later (for argument's sake), modern – or by then 'contemporary' art[7] – had truly become a 'machine' where every component (a work, an artist, an institution, a critical concept…) implied the internal 'workings' of the entire mechanism and in which the function of one part could be deduced from another. But by then, the adventurous machine age was over, displaced by the age of information. The avant-garde left the engine running as it jumped off, just when it seemed that the breaks had failed and the train was heading for the end of the tracks. The machinery of contemporary art seemed to be no longer fuelled by the new. Rather, it seemed to be endlessly replicating the axiomatic *idea* of innovation. And it seemed to be going faster than ever before – so fast that the new seemed to have shattered into a flicker of multiple and simultaneous instants, and it no longer looked like anything we could recognise or agree upon.

5 Robert Hughes, "The Mechanical Paradise", *The Shock of the New*, BBC Books, London, 1980, p.12.

6 Ernst Bloch, the son of a Bavarian railway manager, described this as 'non-synchronism'.

7 As far as I can ascertain, the term 'contemporary art' dates back at least to the late 1910s when it denoted, particularly in Soviet Russia, radical artistic tendencies sensitive to progressive social and political priorities. While since the 1940s the term has been used more liberally, often to encompass all art being produced at the time, or even within a living memory, I take it that in its prevalent usage it has retained something of its original sentiment and that this usage partially overcomes and partially obscures the often diagnosed schism between 'avant-garde art' and the 'critical artistic practices' of recent decades.

8 Robert Adams, 'Making Art New', *Beauty in Photography: Essays in Defense of Traditional Values*, Aperture, New York, 1981, pp 77-8.

Robert Adams resorts to a railway analogy to illustrate his view that in contemporary art, 'novelty is the look-alike for progress.'[8] He recalls how, sometime in the late 1970s, an *Artforum* subscription campaign warned that 'the pace of contemporary art is swift', and adds his own by-line: 'Don't be left behind. All aboard for the art express, bound at dreamlike velocity for unknown lands'. The attitude that provoked Adams' sarcastic remark has become symptomatic of a growing tendency in the post-industrial information society to negotiate the function of 'contemporary' art, the symbolic space it occupies, almost solely against a proliferation and turnover of incidental points of interest. The volatile priorities of momentary attention show through everywhere in magazines and galleries, in art schools and at conferences – and not only within the narrow circles of the custodians and patrons of contemporary art and among the 'trend-spotters' on their perimeters, but also throughout the 'marketplace of culture', in the wider worlds of media and politics.

It is not just the promiscuity of consumer hedonism that should be blamed for this, nor is it only an inevitable consequence of the overproduction of cultural waste typical of the information society (although neither are excused here). Art is of course opportunistic: it is a pursuit of latent possibilities. These possibilities are both practical and theoretical and are limited by the available technological means of production as much as by the cultural conditions that provide art with content, purpose and meaning. The intense competition for a 'contemporary' status (as a desirable option if not an absolute necessity) produces different criteria for change at different times. However, in the main, the self-conscious 'pushing back of limits' and the conquest of the 'unknown lands' has always been above all a matter of what is said rather than what is done. The performative discrepancies between promise and reality, vision and realisation, statement and fact, in art as in the whole of culture, have taken care of this. In 'current' art, at the open end of contemporary art from where art is speaking to 'our times', as it were, the strategic contestation of rhetorical positions has turned into a fracas of isolated academic skirmishes amongst a widely proclaimed plurality of discourses. Meanwhile in the public realm, in the social destination of artists' efforts, the manifestos and proclamations of the avant-garde age have given way to a spectacle of prize giving and media debates in which any arbitrary notion of the 'current' appears to be the critical arbiter of the 'contemporary'. The 'cutting edge', a popular contemporary fiction which still echoes the aspirations of the modernist era, is now marked by randomly dispersed talking points.

*　*　*

Benjamin, Hughes and Adams are unlikely allies. All they share is the use
of a well-established metaphor. And it is perhaps appropriate that it should fall
on Adams, a photographer, to try and put the spanner in the works – just as
it makes sense that it should have been 'the man with a movie camera', Dziga
Vertov, who once cried 'Make way for the machine!', and that it should have been
Andy Warhol, the archetypal 'artist using photography', who in his day seemed
to enjoy the ride so much that he dreamed of becoming a machine himself.

Photography has had a particular place among the complex of cultural
practices that have acted as a catalyst in the rise and decline of the avant-garde
project, and has become a symptom, beneficiary and the most familiar
accomplice of our post-industrial cultural existence. The arguments are well
rehearsed: as a technology of illusion photography has revolutionised the
possibilities of art so radically that the very identity of art has been thrown
into question; as a largely automatic process it has helped to divest art of a
commitment to formal experimentation (and so of its accountability to taste);
as a means of mechanical reproduction, with its accuracy, speed, ease of use
and economy, it has both democratised and compromised the reception of
works of art (with profound consequences for the confidence of the 'trend-
spotter'); in its symbolic function it has facilitated a reciprocity or feed-back
between art and mass culture (which, in turn, has helped to shift attention
from aesthetic considerations to social performance); in its didactic or cognitive
function it has taught us new 'ways of seeing' (and has brought to the fore the
notion of art as a diet for an 'informed' public); and not least, the essential
attachment of the photographic image to the external world has entirely changed
the character of representation (equalising all recordable phenomena whilst
also creating new hierarchies of recorded events).

The co-existence of art and photography within modern visual culture has
itself been a source of instability. The question of whether or not photography
is a continuation of older modes of art or image-making craft has exercised
the minds of many commentators with a strange urgency for the best part of
photography's history. Likewise, the question of art *as* photography has been
fraught with contention. While the arguments and counter-arguments have
never caused much excitement among the practitioners of photography
(including the happily snapping vast majority of people who use and value
photography not for its cultural status but for what it can do) they nevertheless
have had an indirect effect on the public perception of contemporary art, at
least to the extent that their persistence (and utter tedium) have acted as a
backdrop to a sense of incompatibility between the unconcerned everyday
consumption of images and the 'critically informed' way of looking demanded
by art. These debates took something of a turn in the 1960s and 1970s, with

9 Aleksandr Rodchenko, "On Contemporary Photography", *Utopias: Russian Modernist Texts, 1905-1940*, Catriona Kelly (ed.), Penguin Books, London, 1999, p.89.

the rise of overtly conceptual art practices that introduced the nominal differentiation between 'photographers' and 'artists *using* photography', and an eruption of diverse theoretical work that recognised the need to understand photography as photography on its own terms.

For the modernist vanguard, the distinction between 'art photography' and other uses of the technology was far from academic. Aleksandr Rodchenko: 'There are millions of stereotyped photographs floating out there... Landscapes, human heads and naked women are called "art photography", while pictures of current events are called "press photography"'.[9] And it was this *other* photography that 'generated a revolution in photography' from which artists had to learn 'in order to teach people to see from new points of view'. These 'new points of view' were of course an ideological requirement of revolutionary instruction, an aspect of an affiliation of the avant-garde to leftist political ideologies. But taken more soberly, and much less literally, the lessons that photography had to teach art about new points of view from 'without' made it possible for photography to learn from art in turn. Now it seems as if photography wants to have nothing to do with art, least of all with art using photography, and the only guidance it has to offer needs to be inferred from the various degrees to which it resists the condition of 'contemporary' art. New points of view, once the bases of the ideological exchange between photography and art, now frequently make the *reception of photography,* in and by 'contemporary' art merely a matter of unilateral reference.

It goes without saying that photography and art overlap at an instrumental level. Photographers can and do use the tools of their trade to make, among other things, works of art and artists make use of photography to do, *inter alia,* things other than making art.[10] At a conceptual level, however, photography and 'contemporary' art have different interests in 'new points of view'. Both art and photography are, of course, modes of noticing and pointing out new things in the world and both test our view of reality. But where photography learns from art, there it now loses much more than it gains. At its simplest, photography pursues new points of view, actual perspectives, with little or no concession to metaphor and not an inch given to ideology, to draw attention to events in the world. For photography, the new is co-incidental at every step to the selective aims of individual photographs. Art draws attention to 'new points of view', in the sense of an external critical capacity, including those points of view provided by specific photographs, as a pretext for attracting attention to its own currency on which it relies for its 'contemporary' epithet. There is no overlap, only moments of sometimes dramatic, but nearly always involuntary, slippage.

10 It is an interesting thought, albeit for another occasion, that the widespread use of photography may have contributed to the recovery of interest among contemporary artists in directly social, 'non-art' activities.

I am making it sound as though photography and art were equipped with
critical consciousness (they 'learn'; they have 'interests'). And indeed, to the
extent that they represent communities of people, they can be thought of as
self-aware bodies. Even as modes of culture, as I prefer to think of them,
they are saturated, surrounded, supported by and preyed upon by bodies
of criticism and theory which know no higher priority than to make culture
conscious of itself – and us conscious of culture's state of mind. The cacophony
of voices may be confusing, but chaos erupts when metaphors get mixed – or
mixed up in critical intentions.

*   *   *

A concrete, if entirely haphazard, example may help to clarify how we learn
to 'see from new points of view' in the reality of our orchestrated encounters
with art. It is provided by a humble gallery leaflet for an exhibition concerned
with the tendency among certain neo-conceptually inclined artists to deploy,
critically, various tactical means and stylistic conventions of documentary
photography in their work.[11] In this anonymous piece of writing too, we find
ourselves amidst the turbulent currents of 'the new'. This comes as no surprise
since we have become so accustomed to the idea that the almost exclusive role
of art galleries and exhibitions is to present something new that it has become
difficult to propose, or even envisage, alternatives. 'Seeing', however, is something of a hyperbole here. What we are 'looking at', or what is being pointed
to us, is explicitly non-visual – not photographs but a use of photography or a
mode of reception – and this demands that the identity of 'the new' be determined
à priori, in the process of critical interpretation. The principal instrument of
such an operation is the keyword.

A quick quantitative analysis of the condensed description of the curatorial
undertaking in our gallery leaflet, reveals four instances of the words 'question'
and 'questioning'. In the very opening sentence of the short text, we are
informed that the works 'question the genre of documentary photography'.
A couple of paragraphs further on, we read that 'in every case, the position
and the relationship of the photographer is questioned'(sic.).We also learn that
'the exhibition as a whole raises questions as to the activities suggested in the
making of the images'. And finally, we find that the accompanying conference
will 'question the tensions and conflicts which invariably run through
documentary practice'

The depressing familiarity of the jargon, the frequency and ease with
which 'questions' and 'questioning' flow from the writer's pen – or pop up on
the word processor screen, as the case is more likely to have been – indicate
that in their collective presence as an exhibition, or as tokens of an identifiable

11 *Face On*, curated by
Mark Durden and Craig
Richardson, Site Gallery,
Sheffield, 2000. The following
remarks are no reflection on
the exhibition itself.

tendency, these works are separated from their precedents and historical models by a certain critical shift encoded in the language of interpretation. This seems to serve as circumstantial evidence of a 'contemporary' relevance of the artist's use of a sublimated genre of photography through a demonstration of a change in the characteristics of the external critical climate in which their work is received. Here then is a 'new point of view'.

A critical attitude towards older or concurrent (competing) modes of production is one of the most distinctive features of modern art. At its most radical, as for instance in 1960s conceptual art, it was this systematic scrutiny of the traditions and conventions of modernist photography that brought to the fore the possibilities of integrating photography's broader social functions, and particularly perhaps its documentary functions, within art.

For the generation of Victor Burgin, John Hilliard, Keith Arnatt, or further afield Douglas Huebler, Dan Graham, the Bechers or Joseph Kosuth, the critical approach to the photographic image and the conventions of photography was summed up in the keyword 'investigation'. The term (inspired no doubt by the influence of Ludwig Wittgenstein, with some assistance from Walter Benjamin) appears prodigiously in the writings of many of the artists themselves – or occasionally in the titles of their works, as with Kosuth's numbered *Investigations* series – and it reflects accurately both the general critical agendas of conceptual art and its systematic methodologies. It also signals an understanding of the photographic image as a site of information and, by extension, of its communicative role in general.

The generation of their disciples (of whom perhaps my fellow contributor here, Olivier Richon, could be respectfully cited as one) carried on the investigation of the photographic medium and image under the heading of 'inquiry', which together with a host of other terms ('discourse', springs readily to mind) seems to have been imported from French post-structuralist criticism and particularly the work of Roland Barthes, whose writing began to be widely read in English translation in the late 1970s. The new vocabulary perhaps indicates a re-orientation from a close attachment to philosophy towards critical theory, its metaphors and its more literary, if not less formal, discursive manners. It parallels a growing preference for elaborate and highly controlled modes of 'constructed' studio photography and still-life against the 'fast-acting' documentary image.

By now, the critical approach to photography that owes so much to the pioneering efforts of the 1970s conceptual artists and the commitments of their 1980s successors has progressed, or has been critically updated, from 'investigation' through 'inquiry' to 'questioning'.

True, on the one hand, keywords are not much more that fashion accessories. They come and go and their arrivals or departures change little in the ways things are. After all, the words 'investigation', 'inquiry' and 'questioning' are for most practical purposes synonymous and it may seem pedantic to dwell on the subtle semantic differences among them. On the other hand, language has a lot to say about the speaker: it betrays the speaker, it puts the speaker at a mercy of circumstances. What is it then that the language of 'questions' and 'questioning' leaves to us to question? Surely, what we should look at are the ways in which this questioning attitude gives an expression to the times we live in.

In so far as evident changes of vocabulary are always symptomatic of changing cultural conditions, and in so far as they provide points of access to the currency of 'contemporary' art, the vocabulary in question here implies, for one, a kind of a advanced scepticism that we are invited to share. A scepticism that is rooted in the findings of the 1970s 'investigations' but goes a step further than the acknowledgement of lost innocence of the postmodernist decade. Having systematically 'investigated' the means and uses of photography, having developed the terms of our engagement with it through a careful theoretical 'inquiry', we seem to have no choice but to approach photography with caution. Photography has become something of a dubious, questionable medium: we use it, but the other photography out there should only be touched with a critical barge pole. Photography seems to have a 'problem' but won't admit it – a bit of an attitude, really – and so the 'contemporary' problem for art becomes the question of a safe critical distance.[12]

Secondly, asking questions is not only a legitimate occupation for an artist, it is also an unavoidable one. Art gives no answers. All it can do is to pose questions. And it hardly needs stressing that the questions worth asking through photography should concern photography's identity, functions and purpose. The question for an artist using photography is quite clear: what is photography for? Indeed, it is obvious that most photographic work that merits attention is asking precisely this. But questioning as a critical end in itself, putting in doubt without a commitment to uncovering and exploring a sense of possibility, is merely an act of surrender to the way things happen to be.

* * *

In his remarkable book, *Towards a Philosophy of Photography*, Vilém Flusser argues that the post-industrial world is dominated not by machines but apparatuses – such as the camera or the computer, the agencies of the state or the market – which are the expressions of the hidden interests of those who control their inputs and outputs. But since these apparatuses have been

12 This scepticism shows through just as much in the evident urge among many of the critically minded to expand the definition of the 'photographic field' seemingly *ad infinitum*, and is further exemplified by the rarity of finding a student on any art photography course, in the UK at least, who actually takes photographs. I should also like to acknowledge Peter Osborne's comment that 'calling it scepticism is being too kind to it'.

13 Vilém Flusser, *Towards a Philosophy of Photography*, Reaktion Books, London, 2000, p. 35.

14 ibid. p.39.

15 John Berger, 'Understanding a Photograph', *Classic Essays on Photography*, Alan Trachtenberg (ed.), Leete's Island Books, New Haven, 1980, p.293. To squeeze another drop from my railway metaphor, this article 'put Berger on a collision course with a growing number of other writers on photography'. John Tagg, *The Burden of Representation*, Macmillan, London, 1988, p.187.

16 op.cit. pp. 81-2.

designed to operate 'automatically', those who control their external functions are, in effect, controlled by their pre-programmed possibilities. 'To put it another way', he says, 'in the act of photography, the camera does the will of the photographer but the photographer has to will what the camera can do'.[13]

The use of the camera involves a series of quantitative choices: Flusser describes it as a 'doubt made up of points of hesitation'.[14] The doubt, as Flusser uses the term, is characterised by the photographers' 'hesitant' exploration of the multiplicity and equality of the possibilities of the camera program without being conscious of the general consequences of the photographic practice. Even if photographers think that they are acting against the camera program, as Flusser insists they must, their decisions are fixed to it. In this respect, even the free choice of what to photograph is a programmed act. (And so is, I might add, the choice of *when* to press the shutter release that John Berger saw as the invisible 'true content of a photograph', its 'message [which], decoded, means: I have decided that seeing this is worth recording.')[15] And every time a photographer succeeds, against the odds, in realising a possibility not predicted within the camera, the channels of distribution deliver the news of the newly discovered possibility to where it will be used to upgrade the program. With a latent help from the gallerist, editor or critic, the camera always wins.

Against this background, Flusser identifies and builds up a case for a certain kind of 'informative' or 'experimental' photography that deconstructs the 'apparatus' and its programming, so that it may produce 'improbable' images which will generate equally improbable responses on the part of the audience. This experimentation, as a probe into the problems of the 'programming and distribution of information', provides a model for coming to terms with 'the fact that there is no place for freedom within the area of automated, programmed and programming apparatuses'. Yet Flusser also believes that a *critical* solution to the paradox of having to uncover 'the terrible fact of this unintentional, rigid and uncontrollable functionality of apparatuses in order to get hold over them' could show that it is 'nevertheless possible to open up the space for freedom'.[16]

Flusser sees this as a role for philosophy, but it is equally a function of art. It may be a compensatory function, and certainly not a new one, but without rising to the task, any claims to currency and contemporaneity we may make for art will sound hollow. How could art use photography to a more credible purpose? It will take more than increasingly desperate attempts to escape the programmatic nature of photography, or reluctant admissions of the impossibility of ever overcoming the condition of the program. It will certainly take more than the scepticism that I detect in the shift of the critical vocabulary that parallels the developments over three generations of what could be termed self-reflective or conceptual photography (but is more likely to recognise itself today as 'contemporary critical practice'). It will take new viewpoints, but not those that only give us the view of streams of (more or less critical) practices marshalled conveniently into trends so as to make the act of looking redundant from the start.

The limits seem to have been pushed over the 'cutting edge'. But there is no escape from the pressures of the new, the current and the contemporary, by whatever conventions they may be determined, just as there is no escape from language. In accepting this we must remember that criticism, theory or the lowly interpretation, are each engaged in different pursuits from their object. The terms we conventionally use, over familiar as they are, can still help us to see the contemporary relevance of a work of art but they do not constitute it. Rather, it is the ability of a work of art to make us notice the familiar as if for the first time, and our own ability to notice the relevance of it, that makes the work truly contemporary.

'The photograph' is what we make of photography in the absence of photographs. Can we trust language? Do we have a choice? Even at the cost of burdening the critical language that gives us and lives off 'contemporary' art with openly ideological demands, we must insist that it lets art show – not that the machine of art is still running – but that things are still moving on. Rather than asking ourselves rhetorically, 'Where is the photograph?' we must demand to know 'Where are the questions?'

Interfaces

Photographic Soul
Richard Shiff

Classifying [operations] as hand- or machine-work is ... all but meaningless ...
'Handicraft' and 'Hand-made' are historical or social terms, not
technical ones.[1]

The mechanics of vector and raster

Theorists commonly develop fundamental distinctions as a way of analyzing
and categorizing modes of representation. During the early twentieth century,
Heinrich Wölfflin famously contrasted Renaissance linearity with Baroque
colourism.[2] In our present age of electronic communication, an opposition
relevant to video and computer imaging would seem the appropriate device:
vector versus raster. Linear drawing, which establishes continuous contours
and edges, is primarily a vector system; each stroke implies a directional
movement the eye can follow, while what surrounds the stroke remains devoid
of tone and often of signification. A drawing sometimes appears like a free-
floating sign within a surrounding field, the dimensions of which could be
reduced or extended without affecting the communicative potential of the
drawn figure. In contrast, a fully toned painting or photograph is primarily a
raster system. Each element of tonality occupies a position on the organizing
raster, which functions as an invisible grid mapping a continuous field of
illumination; no space within this field remains 'empty'.

I use 'grid' in a general sense to indicate a kind of distribution system.
Neither horizontals nor verticals are required. The raster of a conventional
television screen, for example, consists only of horizontals, which actually
slant at a slight downward angle, left to right. The lack of a vertical component
in the grid doesn't prevent the image from maintaining uniform density.
A picture is virtually present even when a raster is blank, because the sum
of picture units   or picture elements, the 'pixels' — is co-extensive with the
surface. Like light-sensitive photographic film, the pictorial raster merely
awaits its activation, as if its differentiating tonalities were to be projected
from within the surface as much as from without.

If there is 'drawing' in conventional photography, it occurs on an implicitly
gridded surface on which all points are of potentially equal value to the image.

1 David Pye, *The Nature and Art
of Workmanship*, Cambridge
University Press, Cambridge,
1968, pp.9-10 (emphasis
eliminated).

2 Heinrich Wölfflin, *Principles
of Art History*, trans. M. D.
Hottinger, Dover, New York,
1950 (original edition 1915).

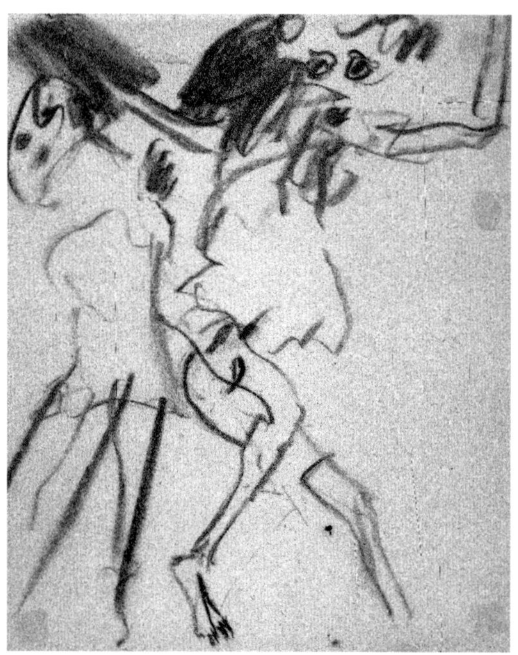

This can also be true of conventional painting, which has a long history of being organized by grids used to aid in tracing images seen through projection devices such as the camera obscura, the camera lucida, and even simple mirrors. The grid also assists in transferring an image freehand from one drawing or painting surface to another.

There are reasons to avoid or subvert the grid, especially in the case of painters who associate line and drawing with their own movements as opposed to a view or projection of something apart from them. In 1966, for example, Willem de Kooning did a series of drawings made with his eyes closed (Figure 13). He imagined the active bodies of others by stretching, compressing, and twisting his own. Working in this manner, de Kooning gave a privileged centrality to all points of contact between his hand and the paper, a type of centrality that a grid or raster would deny. This blind, motion-oriented procedure often resulted in the heads of represented figures striking the edges of the paper, causing the artist to compress that part of the body and render the hair to the side wherever there was room, as if a real body were accommodating its volume to a confining space. Where there was no figure – that is, no drawing – there was also no signification, if only because de Kooning neither saw nor touched these surrounding spaces; they left no impression on him. A camera, however, would sense and register the empty and the full equally, acknowledging and activating the raster.

If de Kooning ignored the raster to free his vectoring hand of its acquired compositional habits, it seems that, for analogous purposes, Chuck Close adopted the raster to suppress the vector. Nearly four decades younger, but active during the same period in which de Kooning was making his drawings with eyes closed, Close let photography provide his initial image, then applied a grid to that source. He became the photographer as well as the painter of his models, as if he were adjudicating between two pictorial authorities, each with its history and claims to a proper image. The interaction he staged in his works of the late 1960s – for example, *Self-Portrait*, 1968 (Figure 14) – stimulated the evolution of both mediums. However automatic and remote photographic technology may be, Close provided it with a high degree of corporeal intimacy: not only a close-up intimacy with the model, but a vision embodied as the artist worked his way through the image in the way de Kooning would work his way through a body (his own as much as his model's). For de Kooning, the artist's body was as much the medium as was graphite, charcoal, or paint. For Close, one medium (painting) became the medium of another (photography). He reproduced by hand an image that had originated in a mechanism, one he himself operated.

Although intimacy, accuracy, and the mechanics of vision – human mechanics as well as machine mechanics – are among Close's continuing artistic interests, he has never sought to test technologies of representation against some putative human standard. Pitting artist against machine hasn't been his concern. Instead he seems to test each of his two mediums, to see what each can do. Around 1967, dissatisfied with his own early, de Kooning-like style of gestural expressionism, Close forced himself to shift to a black-and-white photographic realism: 'I found it incredibly liberating to make very neat, precise paintings... I was trying to make my work look like photographs in order to get my hand out of there, because I had all of these habits that were associated with other people's work. I was trying to purge de Kooning ...'[3] There are vectors in Close's work just as there are in other handmade paintings – strokes that convey meaning as directional indicators – yet Close is primarily a raster artist. With a raster, he 'purged' de Kooning.

In his recent paintings Close leaves the grid boldly visible; rather than a mere guide for transference (as in *Self-Portrait*), it becomes a pictorial element in itself. Its activity extends to areas where nothing is being depicted other than a quality of blank light or empty space. A brilliantly colored work like *Emma*, 2000 (Figure 15), is very much alive with variation in the nominally

3 Chuck Close, quoted in Robert Storr, 'Interview with Chuck Close' (1997), *Chuck Close*, The Museum of Modern Art, New York, 1998, p.95; 'Chuck Close, conversation with Roy Lichtenstein', 23 October 1995, in Joanne Kesten, ed., *The Portraits Speak*, A.R.T. Press, New York, 1997, p.619.

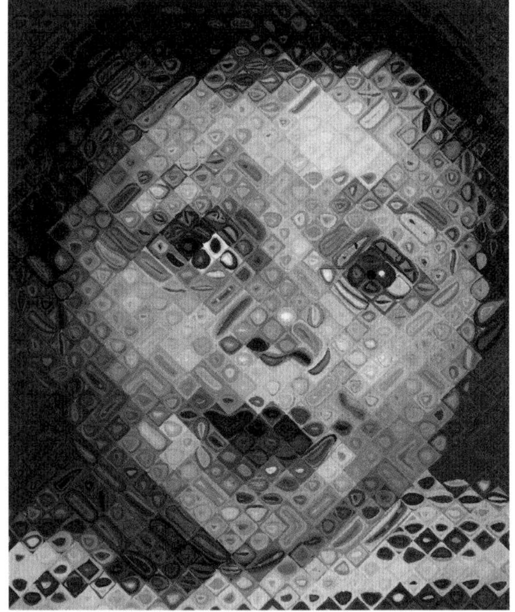

4 Chuck Close, statement to
the author, 1997.

5 Chuck Close, in Kirk Varnedoe,
ed., *Artist's Choice: Chuck Close*,
The Museum of Modern Art,
New York, 1991, 7. An 'instant',
of course, is not no time, but
imperceptible time.

recessive areas of the raster. Out to the very edges, Close's surface tenses with tones of warm and cool that reverse to cool and warm. From a distance these variations cancel out and may seem to combine into uniformity. Yet Close's backgrounds are never at rest: they consume nearly as much material substance and creative energy as the more elaborate configurations that correspond to eyes and lips; they feature the featureless. Because of the nature of the mechanism, the same could be said of the kind of conventional photography that Close uses as his source.

Close once said of his early works in black-and-white (made largely with an airbrush) that they looked as if the filmy image had 'moved in on a fog and [fallen] into the painting.'[4] With this all-at-once quality, Close's paintings of the late 1960s give the stilled appearance of a photograph. But this is deceptive since these two raster mediums diverge in a manner the artist himself has articulated: 'A photograph is complete in an instant, but a painting is incomplete until it is finished; with a painting, each thing you add changes what is already there.'[5] The difference depends on successive actions of the hand, which, unlike fog or photochemistry, follow the vagaries of intuitive judgment. The artist adjusts and fine-tunes his elements in a play that approaches traditional composition, but at an unfamiliar level of resolution: hair by hair, pore by pore,

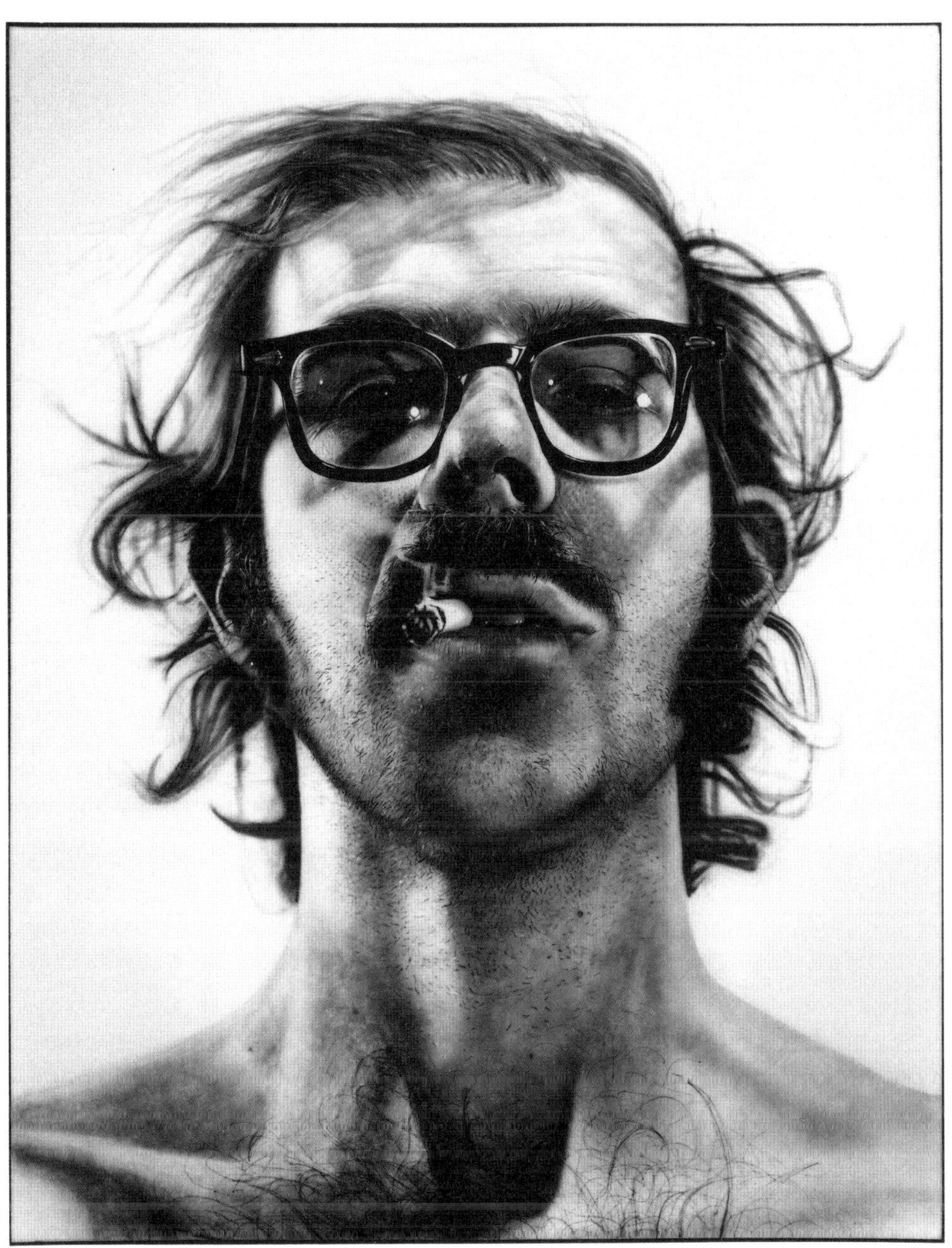

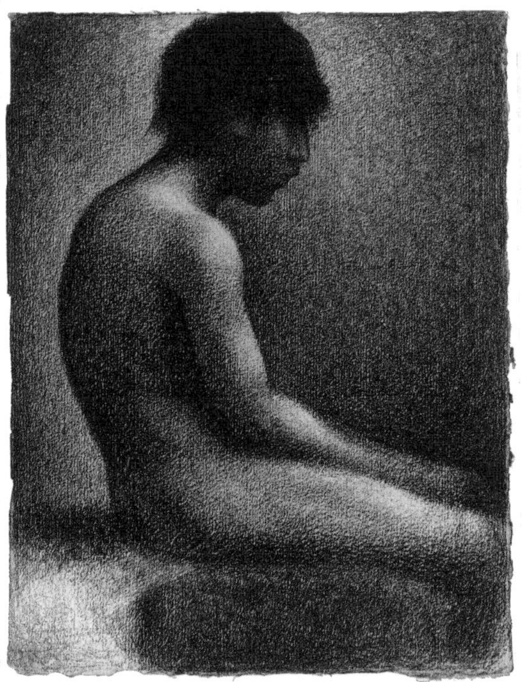

6 Chuck Close quoted in Patrick Pacheco, 'Point Counterpoint', *Art & Antiques*, 8 October 1991, p.73.

mark by barely perceptible mark. This is why the images in Close's paintings are so arresting, beyond the fascination of their rigorous handwork. To the unwary, the differences between his photograph of his model and the corresponding painting remain subliminal – like subtle variations in the nuanced look on a living human face to which one responds without knowing why.

Close has described the black-and-white conté crayon drawings of Georges Seurat as a parallel to his own early paintings, a kind of fog setting in: 'While you're aware of the making, the artist's hand has almost disappeared. [Seurat's] drawings are almost apparitions. You're not quite sure where the edge is' (Figure 16).[6] The description suggests that Seurat's drawings resemble photographs; in particular, photographs in the process of development. They just appear, magically. To put it another way, Seurat was making raster drawings, the antithesis of what de Kooning was doing. A fog may well be a better metaphor than an apparition, because its evocation of movement captures what distinguishes painting and drawing from photography, at least for artists who translate one medium into the other. As Close stated, a typical painting is done slowly, adding part to part, and each addition responds to elements already there. This amounts to a process of continuous approximation, averaging out, adjustment.

Seurat is a predecessor for artists who self-consciously link the character of their imagery to the medium that generates it. To many of his contemporaries, his art appeared depersonalized and mechanical, an objection some now raise against Close. During Seurat's lifetime there seem to have been three fundamental considerations applied to the critique of his painting. These might also be addressed to photography, and often were. First: Could it be concluded that Seurat's procedure was redeemed by its 'science' – was it true to natural fact, objective, and potentially of universal application? Second: Would the constraints and discipline of that procedure encourage or inhibit individual vision and expression? And finally: Would Seurat's method result in a superior product – a representation achieving not only precision but beauty and grace, perhaps because its own mechanicity allowed it to avoid all stylistic pretence? One early critic wrote that Seurat's method 'left to each [artist] his personality while mechanically obtaining the most forceful effect.'[7] But another worried that the new technique was becoming far too 'mechanical' in the hands of the artist's followers.[8]

Photography, soul, animation

These central issues of nineteenth-century painting – its realism, its expressiveness, its science, its aestheticism – accord with those that critics applied to photography during its early reception. The context is clearest with regard to the representation of landscape in the two mediums. Reviewing the Salon of 1847, the French art critic Paul Mantz argued that landscape painters who naively concentrated on observing what they saw, restricting themselves to registering the image, would inevitably introduce their expressive personalities. Mantz referred to the trace of the individual as something that would quietly 'slip into' the picture, most likely as some characteristic idiosyncrasy in paint handling.[9] He implied that the more intensely and scrupulously, hence objectively and even mechanically, a painter observed a given site, the more subjective the picture might become.

A second reviewer of the same Salon of 1847, Théophile Thoré, recommended that the artist limit initial action to a certain recognition: 'Nature [itself] assumes the role of composing images, fully ready to be reproduced in a form of art. A landscapist stops along a forest path and finds a complete picture right on the spot, with a central effect and well-organized lines. [The landscapist] has only to paint what has been made directly by nature.'[10] This was Thoré's way of asserting that painters could prosper in the absence of

7 Thadée Natanson, 'Un primitif d'aujourd'hui: Georges Seurat', *La revue blanche*, 21, 15 April 1900, pp.612-13. Here and elsewhere, unless otherwise noted, my translation.

8 Gustave Geffroy, 'Indépendants', *Revue d'aujourd'hui*, 1, 15 April 1890, p.270.

9 'In landscape naively studied, without the preoccupation of style, a highly poetic element, which traditional [academic methods] will not admit, can slip in [*se glisser*] – this is the personality of the artist'; Paul Mantz, *Salon de 1847*, Ferdinand Sartorius, Paris, 1847, p.96. Mantz's argument was quite common then, as it continues to be now.

10 Thoré-Bürger (Théophile Thoré), 'Salon de 1847', *Les Salons*, 3 vols., Lamertin, Brussels, 1893, 1, p.538. Thoré's statement is embedded in his commentary on the sculpture of Jean-Baptiste Clésinger: 'A sculptor has his [female] model assume a pose and suddenly a contour appears, exalting and impassioning him. The statue is done. It remains only to disengage this figure from a block of marble', (pp.538-39). Thoré, however, was not advocating slavish copying; he praised Clésinger for editing out insignificant details as he proceeded.

authoritative antecedents, without the traditions and conventions associated with an aristocratic social order and the teachings of its schools, without a set of preconditions for representational expression. Facing nature, painters would discover a 'complete picture', superior to any work of academic invention. Nature's image – self-composed, as it were – offered the advantage of liberating the artist from established expressive paradigms, just as Close's raster had liberated him from de Kooning's vector.

When Thoré wrote on art he wasn't merely concerned with personal achievement but with the nature of his society. He wanted the value judgments of artists to be those of politically autonomous individuals, guided by their immediate experience. The strict reproduction of a view given to the senses would represent an original artistic thought, a corrective to the intellect and the imagination, which would otherwise follow only ideologically sanctioned channels. Artists encountering a sensory actuality would resist inherited authoritarian orders that worked to shape lives and responses in advance of experience. Thoré's position established both an empirical ideal and an expressive one; the two combine in what nineteenth-century critics called 'realism'.[11] Photographers could create realism, and so could painters.

Not surprisingly, the usual signs of an artist's commitment to realism – attention to the mundane; the adoption of a straightforward and even awkward style; naive, rudimentary design – came under suspicion as mere Romantic *affectations*, moves as calculated as any academic mannerism.[12] It might be argued that Seurat systematized his art precisely to eliminate affectation, that Close employed the grid to avoid his affectation of de Kooning's gestures, and that de Kooning himself developed his awkward technique of drawing with eyes closed in order to escape the affectations of his incomparible facility.[13]

In several essays of around 1810, which now seem prophetic, Heinrich von Kleist provided an early modern analysis of affectation. He wrote of it as the consequence of a mislocated soul. Because the soul functions to keep body and mind coordinated and regulated, its displacement causes the mechanism of the body, or of any organism, or even of a machine (at least metaphorically) to lose its natural grace and beauty of performance. A body having an inoperative soul becomes affected and artificial – mechanistic as opposed to mechanical.[14] It moves, but without efficiency and evident purpose. A machine in good working order is analogous to a body with a proper soul. Like a well-regulated painting by Seurat, a machine will appear mechanistic only when it malfunctions; otherwise, it exhibits grace and beauty.

It should be obvious at this point that, in many respects, the mechanical nature of the new medium of photography entailed no disadvantage:

11 Compare Richard Shiff, 'Art History and the Nineteenth Century: Realism and Resistance', *Art Bulletin*, 70, March 1988, pp.31-33.

12 Champfleury (Jules Fleury), *Histoire de l'imagerie populaire*, Dentu, Paris, 1886 (original edition 1869), p.xlvi: 'One does not learn naiveté. Naiveté comes from the heart, not the brain'. The educator Ludovic Vitet warned of 'intentional and systematic naiveté' (See 'Eustache Lesueur,', Revue des deux mondes, 27, 1 July 1841, p.58). The Romantic-modernist issue of artificial naiveté had been articulated by Immanuel Kant (See *The Critique of Judgment* [1790], trans. James Creed Meredith, Oxford University Press, Oxford, 1952, pp.166-67) and Friedrich Schiller (See *On the Naive and Sentimental in Literature* [1795-96], trans. Helen Watanabe-O'Kelley, Carcanet New Press, Manchester, 1981), as well as, somewhat later, Heinrich von Kleist (see below).

13 On the last point, see Richard Shiff, 'The Gravity of Willem de Kooning's Twist', in Enrique Juncosa and Teresa Millet, eds., *Willem de Kooning*, IVAM, Valencia, 2001, pp.54-89.

14 Heinrich von Kleist, 'On the Puppet Theater' (1810), in Philip B. Miller, ed. and trans., *An Abyss Deep Enough: Letters of Heinrich von Kleist with a Selection of Essays and Anecdotes*, Dutton, New York, 1982, p.213.

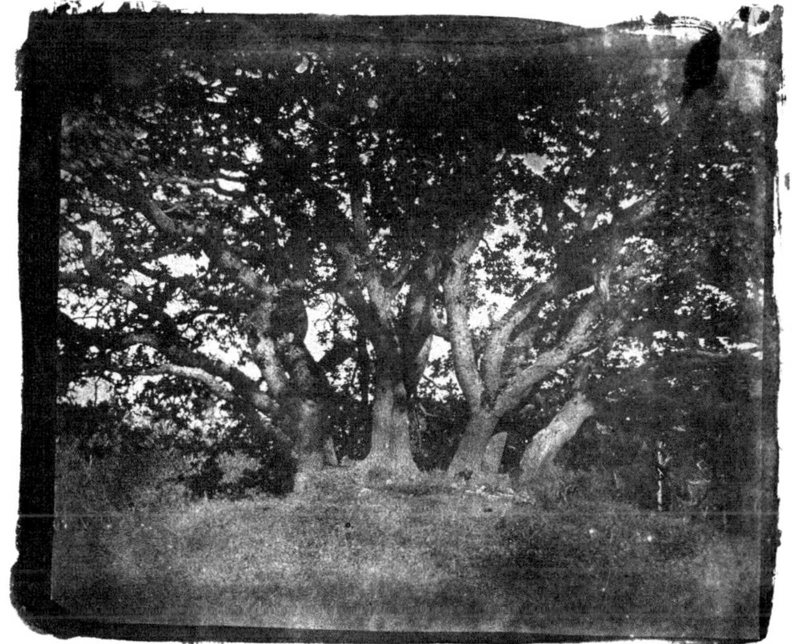

Figure 17. William Henry Fox Talbot, *Oak Tree in Carclew Park*, c.1841.

photography was remarkably efficient. It functioned well. It therefore had naturalness and grace. Moreover, as an operation largely immune to human interference, it afforded little opportunity for the artistic affectation and self-consciousness that would spoil the truth of its image. William Henry Fox Talbot, inventor of the calotype process, argued that his new medium would extend the qualities of existing modes of representation, not undermine them: 'Even the accomplished artist will call in sometimes this auxiliary aid, when pressed for time in sketching a building or a landscape, or when wearied with the multiplicity of its minute details.'[15] The capacity of photography to capture detail presented no threat to creativity. It merely provided an enhanced field of aesthetic nuance. Thoré argued that nature itself did this, if only the artists would look. Photography facilitated their looking.

> The speculations of Fox Talbot's friend George Butler in 1841 are relevant:
> *What I should like to see, would be a set of photogenic Calotype drawings of Forest Trees, the Oak, Elm, Beech etc. taken, of course, on a perfectly calm day, when there should not be one breath of wind to disturb and smear-over the outlines of the foliage. This would be the greatest stride towards effective drawing and painting that has been made for a Century. One Artist has one touch for*

15 H. F. Talbot, 'Calotype (Photogenic) Drawing', *Literary Gazette*, 13 February 1841, p.108.

16 George Butler, letter to Fox Talbot, 25 March 1841, quoted in Larry J. Schaaf, *The Photographic Art of William Henry Fox Talbot*, Princeton University Press, Princeton, 2000, p.150 (emphasis eliminated).

17 H. F. Talbot, op.cit., p.108.

18 Butler, letter to Talbot, 25 March 1841, in Schaaf, op.cit, p.150.

19 Francis Wey, 'De l'influence de l'héliographie sur les beaux-arts', *La lumière*, 9 February 1851, p.2.

20 It was argued that through the new medium of photography, the accuracy of past artistic representations of the human passions was being scientifically confirmed – in photography, art and science converged; Yves Guyot, 'L'art et la science', *Revue scientifique*, 14, 30 July 1887, pp.139-40, p.145.

21 The modern form of this notion is Cartesian, with its radical differentiation of soul from matter and materiality; see René Descartes, 'Discourse on Method' (1637), *Philosophical Writings*, ed. and trans. Norman Kemp Smith, Modern Library, New York, 1958, p.119. For a contrary view, on the materiality of the soul, see Julien Offray de La Mettrie, 'Treatise on the Soul' (1745), *Machine Man and Other Writings*, ed. and trans. Ann Thomson, Cambridge University Press, Cambridge, 1996, pp.65-66. On ancient views of the soul, see Aristotle, *De anima*, and Plato, *Phaedrus*, 245e.

foliage, another has another; and we may from such characteristic touch divine the intended tree and perhaps name the Artist. But your photogenic drawing would be a portrait; it would exhibit the touch of the great Artist, Nature... What a beautiful Set of Studies of Trees... might thus be prepared in a very short time![16]

Apparently, early photographers believed that the new medium had at least two advantages over conventional drawing by hand. First, it produced accurate, detailed images with relatively little effort – provided that nature cooperated by offering a model like an oak tree on a calm day, already as still as the photograph that would picture it (Figure 17). Talbot's initial mix of chemicals used in the calotype process required a relatively long exposure, so blurring could be a problem. Second (and this would be controversial), photography eliminated the individualizing trace of the artist. It seemed to Butler that with the calotype, nature alone would construct the image, as if a tree like the oak were to cast its reflection or its trace upon the photographic film. Talbot nevertheless resisted the fear that photography would 'substitut[e] mere mechanical labor in lieu of talent and experience'; there was 'ample room for the exercise of skill and judgment' because the human operator would control certain variations, such as those produced by differences in the exposure time.[17] Butler, like Talbot, never assumed that photography would displace handwork; instead, it would instruct. Artists would copy photographs, gaining 'facility and accuracy and decision in the characterizing of trees and [in] delineating their respective foliage.'[18]

A decade later in 1851, Francis Wey extended the human factor further into the photographic medium. He argued that the soft-focus calotype print was particularly effective in 'animating' the camera image and affording 'the expression of feeling.'[19] Wey's term 'animate' (*animer*) is crucial. It connotes organic movement and the breath, spirit, or soul that would motivate the living force. The *anima* is indeed the soul, and (as Kleist and others believed) the soul is the source of movement or motivation in a body. The capacity for 'feeling', rather than the degree of visual accuracy or nuance, was the issue on which photographic representation and that of any other medium would rise or fall, at least in its artistic, as opposed to scientific, use.[20] To represent 'feeling' a medium had to accommodate a 'soul'. It seems that souls communicated best with other souls, and that a medium either devoid of soul or insensitive to it might interfere with the process. Prevailing opinion was that sentient beings possessed souls, but matter and machines did not, other than metaphorically.[21] Some commentators explicitly denied photography a soul, alluding not only to its mechanicity but to the character of its material trace – a surface unnaturally and inorganically regularized (as, a generation later, Seurat's painting surface would seem to be). Observing a photograph, 'we feel that the hand, or rather the soul, is absent', wrote Henri Delaborde in 1856.[22] 'Imperfections contribute to give [works of the hand] individuality – as it were, a soul', Ernest Chesneau argued in 1880, as a French admirer of John Ruskin.[23] Was the photographic image too 'perfect' perhaps because it was so still? Although it could express the character of its operator, the photographic medium produced a raster-image with little trace of any animating vector. It lacked a 'hand'.

Ironically, there proved to be a mechanical, as opposed to a manual, way of enhancing the liveliness of photography, and this was simply to animate it and give it movement, as was done in the photographic sequences or chronophotography produced by the American Eadweard Muybridge and the Frenchman Etienne Jules Marey. Film projection was soon to follow and, appropriately, its early name was 'animated photography' – that is, either moving photography or photography-with-a-soul (depending on the critical perspective).[24] The mechanics of film were unusually complicated and only slowly perfected. One of the problems was the material interference known as 'flicker'; it was caused by the eye's ghostly registration of the action of the shutter, a 'rapid alternation of extreme light [shutter open] and extreme dark [shutter closed]', as each still frame was shifted into position before the projection lens.[25] Perhaps flicker itself was the sign of the soul of the medium, a quality of illumination belonging to the machine rather than the image. The severity of flicker varied in relation to the type of shutter used, as well as to the distribution of light and dark in the scene being projected. The phenomenon of flicker, which irritates and fatigues the eye, is a dramatic instance of the tension between the material features of the medium and its representational function of conveying an image. When early projectionists attempted to eliminate flicker by using no shutter at all 'rain' appeared – a different mani-festation of the 'persistence of vision' – that resulted from the dark-to-light contrast in the succession of projected images rather than from the repeatedly interrupted beam of projected light.[26] The medium had not yet attained sufficient transparency or silence for only an image to remain; it had what we call visual 'noise'.

Flicker was eventually eliminated by reducing the time in which a single frame of a filmstrip would be projected without a break in the beam of light. The time during which the image was visible was made equal to the time it wasn't visible – and *that* time had been determined by what was required for the image to be switched to the next frame in the animated mechanical sequence.[27] This suggests that time as well as the spatial field of the picture was becoming regularized, averaged-out, and grid-like, with the moments

22 Henri Delaborde, 'La photographie et la gravure' (1856), *Mélanges sur l'art contemporain*, Renouard, Paris, 1866, p.371, p.373.

23 Ernest Chesneau, *The Education of the Artist*, trans. Clara Bell, Cassell, London, 1886 (original edition 1880), p.257.

24 See Cecil M. Hepworth, *Animated Photography: The ABC of the Cinematograph*, ed. Hector MacLean, Hazell, Watson & Viney, London, 1900. Frederick A. Talbot (*Moving Pictures: How They Are Made and Worked*, William Heinemann, London, 1912, p.7) noted appropriately that 'animated photography is not animation [actual movement] at all'. The process that came to be called 'animation' (conventionally animated film) involves drawing by hand in addition to photography and therefore has a strong vector component, itself a form of animation. Digital, computer-assisted animation complicates this already complicated medium.

25 Hepworth, op.cit., pp.52-58, pp. 112-13; F. A. Talbot, op.cit., pp.88-95.

26 Hepworth, ibid, pp.54-55.

27 See E. G. Lutz, *Animated Cartoons*, Charles Scribner's Sons, New York, 1920, pp.12-13.

28 For examples of test patterns
and types of interference,
see John R. Meagher and Art
Liebscher, *TV Servicing*, Radio
Corporation of America,
Harrison NJ, 1951. A functional
definition of 'noise' is provided
by Abraham Moles, *Information
Theory and Esthetic Perception*,
trans. Joel E. Cohen, University
of Illinois Press, Urbana, 1966,
p.79: 'A noise is a signal that
the sender does not want
to transmit'.

29 See Vladimir K. Zworykin
and George A. Morton,
*Television: The Electronics of
Image Transmission in Color and
Monochrome*, Wiley, New York,
1954, pp.203-4.

empty of image becoming equal partner to the moments full of image. A kind of proto-digitation applied to time is the result. We think of the bit-by-bit paintings of Close and also of Seurat: whereas their works distribute images in space, the mechanical cinematic raster (independent of the photographic component of the film strip) distributes an image in time.

Somewhat after the development of cinema, broadcast radio would have its various forms of audible static and, still later, television its visible forms of interference – waves, distortion, 'snow' – which technology would work to eliminate, as if to perfect the medium. A pattern of waves across a television screen indicates a conflict between electronic signals, one informational sign competing with another. Television test patterns were devised to diagnose the source of any interference according to distortions visible in differently configured areas of the fixed image. As a broadcast the geometric test pattern itself provides no particular information – it does not move – until alien electronic 'noise' interferes. The noise then becomes the information, perhaps even the sign of a soul, useful to the diagnostic engineer whose concern is to restore the medium to its proper silence, so its projected broadcast image will once again come in line with a normative raster.[28] In conventional North American television, soon to be obsolete, the raster consists of a pattern of 525 horizontal lines that the scanner follows as it creates the picture by projecting a sequential beam of electrons, activating numerous momentary bursts of phosphorescence. The raster is conceived as a passive element in the operation; yet its structure, intended to be invisible at normal viewing distance (beyond the eye's capacity to discern it), sets material and physical limitations to the medium – for instance, the degree of resolution in the image, of which the fixed number of lines in the raster is a factor.[29]

In the case of rapidly flashing particles of 'snow' (a non-filmic flicker), interference is generated from 'inside' the television apparatus. 'Snow' can be caused by random weak signals that interfere with the dominant signal, but it becomes especially evident when the set receives only weak signals or no signal at all. In response, the amplifier seeks out a strong signal or any signal. In lieu of anything better, the receiving medium will produce a transient moving pattern of its own upon the raster – variations in illumination at or near the scale of the individual pixel, patterns which never coalesce into an intelligible 'picture'. Even without a broadcast signal and consequent image the screen does not become dark. A play of void and phosphorescence animates it, an interference that interferes with nothing. In a reversal familiar to modern painters, this material assertion of the medium becomes the 'image' (hence our use of the metaphor 'snow', which paradoxically evokes a referent in nature). The effect actively represents the medium as it represents itself in its sensate condition of being 'on', responding to the ambient electronic environment.[30] The medium gives an electronic sign of 'life', analogous to a pulse, breath, or quiver, as if possessing a soul. Is the pictorial result an imperfection – or rather a phenomenon of aesthetic interest, beauty and grace?

Testing history

Consider the historical sequence of mediums from painting (or murals, painting's more public manifestation), to photography (or illustrated magazines and billboards), to film (or cinema), to video (or television), to digital conversions of each of these types of representation. Such a sequence implies that the materiality of visual imagery has decreased to the extent that it hardly remains a factor in communication.[31] With the newer modes of representation, it seems that we rarely confront the physicality of an expressive hand and soul. (The current vogue for fast cutting, slow motion, and jarring, high-volume sound in artists' videos may be an attempt – nostalgic in its way – to call docile senses to attention, restoring sensitivity to an interventive human touch.)

The history of the reception of Seurat's art reflects the twentieth-century technological shift in expectations. With ever less materiality to engage viewers, people detect it where it previously went unnoticed. What once appeared dehumanized and 'mechanical' because it lacked the usual signs of manual flourish, acquires something of an archaic or atavistic human quality due to the mere fact of its individualized hand labor.[32] With a sense of technological crisis (and a bit of rhetorical panic), Meyer Schapiro in 1957 called painting and sculpture 'the last hand-made, personal objects within our culture.'[33]

One thing is evident: over the years, Seurat came to appear increasingly as a painter of the pure mark, that is, of 'nothing'. By nothing, I mean *images* of nothing. To many critics living through the earlier years of the ascendancy of film, radio, and television, it seemed that Seurat produced paintings in which the material display of the medium became more involved and informative than the represented character of the scene. The more the local structure of Seurat's image approached the preexisting condition of the raster, the more it looked like nothing at all. The analogy to interference in a test pattern, and also to flicker or snow, is obvious. Seurat's 'nothing' was most apparent in his summer paintings of seacoasts, which contain expanses of sand, water, and sky rendered with an ever varied pattern of dots – a 'sensation of the visual void', commented one early critic.[34] 'Who before Seurat ever conceived exactly the pictorial possibilities of empty space?' Roger Fry asked later; 'his pictures

30 On 'receiver noise' and 'snow' see Zworykin and Morton, op.cit, p.182, p.720. On a minimum signal see M. A. Krupnick, *The Electric Image: Examining Basic TV Technology*, Knowledge Industry Publications, White Plains, 1990, p.10.

31 A case of the tension between mediums within this historical sequence: trying to reproduce a projected film with a television camera, Philo T. Farnsworth removed the shutter (designed to compensate for the essential discontinuity of the film image) in an attempt to coordinate the continuous electromechanical scanning of the television camera with a corresponding *appearance* of continuity in the action recorded mechanically on the film; see David E. Fisher and Marshall Jon Fisher, *Tube: The Invention of Television*, Oxford University Press, Oxford, 1996, p.162. Film and video possess both analog and digital features but in very different respects.

32 Initially, critics emphasized that regardless of the subject rendered, Seurat's 'handling of the brush remains the same' and that with pointillism "manual facility becomes a negligible matter": Félix Fénéon, Les impressionnistes en 1886, 'L'Impressionnisme' (1887), reprinted in Joan U. Halperin, ed., *Félix Fénéon: Oeuvres plus que complètes*, 2 vols., Droz, Geneva, 1970, 1: p.36, p.67.

33 Meyer Schapiro, 'The Liberating Quality of Avant-garde Art', Artnews, 56, Summer 1957, p.38.

34 Paul Adam, 'Peintres impressionnistes' (1886), reprinted in Ruth Berson, ed., *The New Painting: Impressionism 1874-1886, Documentation*, 2 vols., Fine Arts Museums of San Francisco, San Francisco, 1996, 1:p.430. Nevertheless, the patterning of Seurat's individual marks (as opposed to their scale and distribution) usually alludes to linear contour. His is a vector system as much as a true raster system but approaches the regularity of the latter.

35 Roger Fry, 'Seurat' (1926), *Transformations*, Doubleday, Garden City, 1956, 250-51. André Lhote, (*Seurat*, Braun, Paris, 1948, p.8) wrote similarly that Seurat's small studies were 'sometimes about nothing'.

36 Meyer Schapiro, 'Seurat and "La Grande Jatte"', *The Columbia Review*, 17, November 1935, p.9; 'New Light on Seurat', *Artnews*, 57, April 1958, p.44. Schapiro expressed his attitude toward television and other electronic arts of 'communication' in 'The Liberating Quality of Avant-garde Art', op.cit., p.40.

37 As if to assert the presence of the brown panel as both the image and its interference, Seurat added a brown hue to his palette mixtures, creating a tension between brown as materialized figuration and brown as material support. Compare Robert L. Herbert, *Georges Seurat 1859-1891*, The Metropolitan Museum of Art, New York, 1991, p.246.

are alive, but not with the life of nature'.[35] Perhaps they are alive like photography and video – animated by the soul of the medium.

Schapiro – for whom it was not pointillism that leveled visual experience into nothingness, but radio and television – claimed that no one could rightfully consider 'Seurat's touch mechanical'; rather it was flexible, varied and responsive.[36] Schapiro might have taken a broader view of the 'mechanical', which need not be so definitively opposed to the organic. For those who have stared at video screens it may seem that both the (active) materiality and the (passive) mechanicity of Seurat's art derived from his acknowledgment of a governing raster as much as from the sensitivity of his moving hand. Not only did he tend to lay out his dots of colour in a pixeled manner, but he also exploited the ground or raster as something that must have material features of its own. This is particularly evident in a number of his small panels, such as his *Study for 'The Shore at Bas-Butin, Honfleur'*, 1886 (Figure 18). It is a seascape, but also an image of 'nothing'. Here, and in a number of related works, Seurat chose to use a panel noticeably roughened with tiny grooves or striations, the equivalent of a preexisting painterly texture or 'touch'. His dabs of paint, especially when applied horizontally to represent the sea, skip over the depressed grooves, leaving an extremely thin, but visible vertical trace, which reveals the natural colour of the wood.[37] These verticals cluster along the horizon line, as if to accentuate this central pictorial feature. Also appearing in the sea, they seem to represent the choppiness of waves, an effect Seurat created in larger paintings by setting vertical dabs against his horizontal, ellipsoidal dots. Granted, the textured ground contributes to representing the seascape image; but more is at stake. The vertical grooves, as a kind of cross-graining, collude with the natural horizontal grain to establish a virtual grid – a raster – in the wood itself: the same type of grid one would imagine as the organizing principle or conceptual reality of the rectangular format. Here, ideality and materiality converge. Seurat's use of this grid acknowledges both the form and the physical substance of the wood panel, the latter manifested initially by the presence of the grooves. In turn, the grid or raster made visible by Seurat's handling of paint structures his image, which thus acquires – the artist seems to acknowledge – the properties of whatever medium facilitates its representational being.

In Seurat's era it was possible to believe that a handicraft medium like painting might still dominate a technological medium like photography in its appeal to the cultural imagination. Commentators of the time certainly made this argument, and a later version of it appears in Schapiro's writings. To the contrary, for those who thought that Seurat's imagery suffered under the influences of science and technology, he looked mechanical, as if he had

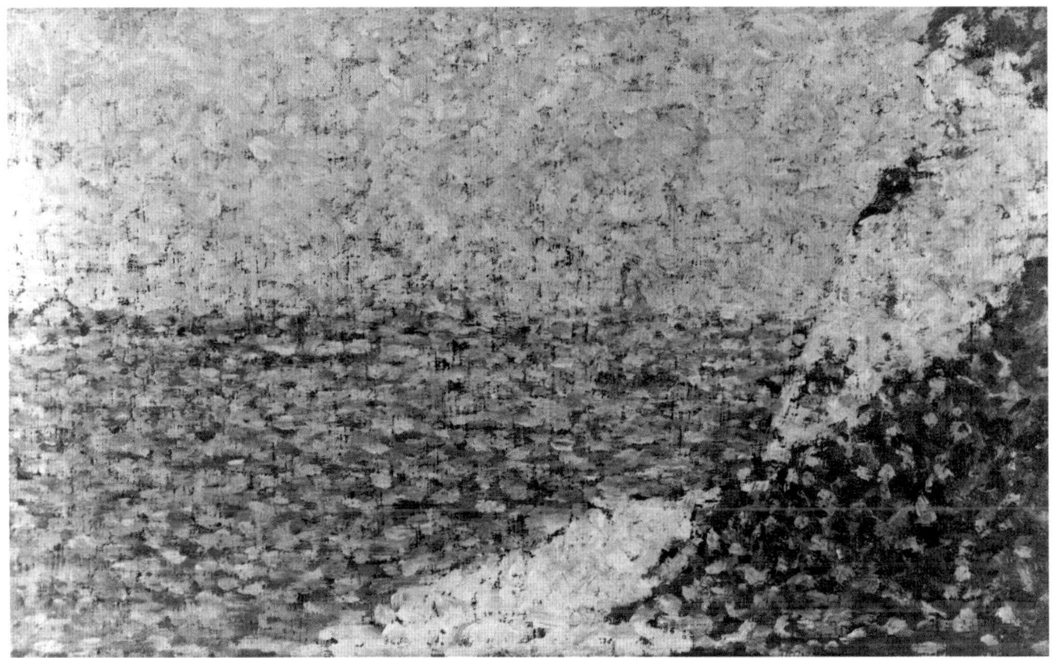

sacrificed his humanity to gain efficiency. Most likely, Seurat believed he was
abandoning only affectation, the effect of a mislocated soul. Now, when the
dominant imagery is electronic and the electronic is digitized – when even the
materiality of television interference is being eliminated – Seurat's art offers
glimpses of the medium at work, insights into persistent factors of material
resistance. He shows that the materiality of the medium remains in force even
when the constituent mark of the image approaches the zero-degree of both
reference and self-referentiality – when the mark lacks pronounced variation,
direction, and character, neither describing externals nor drawing attention
to itself. At whatever size, Seurat's pixel-like dot never truly recedes from
view. More than merely facilitating representation, it marks representation's
material limit.

In a comprehensive theory of art which Seurat read, Charles Blanc wrote
in 1867: 'The painter's touch will always be good if it is natural, that is, if
it follows his heart'.[38] One would think that following the heart is entirely
different from following a raster. But is it? When Wey claimed to find animation
in photography, he need not have stressed the nuanced blur of the calotype
print with its visual resemblance to heartfelt handwork. In fact, animation

Figure 18. Georges Seurat,
*Preparatory sketch for the
painting La Greve Du Bas-Butin,
Honfleur*, 1886.

38 Charles Blanc, *Grammaire
des arts du dessin*, Henri
Laurens, Paris, 1880 (original
edition 1867), p.578.

39 André Lhote, *Traité du paysage*, Floury, Paris, 1939, p. 31.

could be 'mechanical' and yet seem entirely true to nature – so true that a separate category of artificial animation finds no use. The term 'animation' has lost all metaphorical application. By a fluid metonymy, it applies as literally to machines as to people, regardless of one's position on the question of 'soul'. A heartbeat is not only 'natural' but also regular and automatic, both like a mechanism and like an artist's systematic variations. Painter André Lhote stated in 1939: 'This veritable mechanism – light on dark, dark on light – animates all great traditional landscapes'.[39] He could have been talking about photography.

In photographic imaging of all sorts, we consider as automatic whatever occurs in the period during which light is allowed to strike the photosensitive surface. We attribute objectivity to the representation that results, relative, of course, to the specifications of the apparatus. Does it matter that the device has a human operator with past experiences and expectations for the future – implying a certain psychological momentum, direction, and vectoring? Perhaps we can ascertain very little of what would predict, or bear upon, the chance moment of indexical registration, production, or creation (the choice of terms is ideological). We nevertheless hardly hesitate to interpret events along at least three parallel paths of historical determination, which, like modes of representation in conflict, produce confounding interference patterns.

First, as critics and theorists, we understand the operation of a particular medium as an autonomous, self-reflexive system with its own inherent tendencies. We argue that the referential meaning of a painting, photograph, or video image depends on conventions of representation established by other images within the same or an allied medium. Second, as individuals living out our own personal histories, we regard the creative play of an artist, relatively isolated in a studio, as an autonomous system of a similar sort, with each new work being a response to that same artist's preceding works. Third, as political entities, we tend to view the entire society, even in its globalization, as if it too were a hermetic environment, with both its ideology and its technology, or the technocratic collusion of the two, acting to contain and suppress human agency.

The belief that agency must be subordinate to historical conditions and forces is, needless to say, as disabling as it is commonplace – a willful, mytho-logical check on an older mythology of heroic individual action. Displacing the old, the new belief generates raster-like, structural accounts of social and political conditions, with events having multiple potential causes, often unfathomable and consistent with descriptive metaphors such as grid, web, text, and rhizome. Lewis Mumford expressed a version of the conceptual syndrome in 1964: 'The center of authority in [a technological society] is no longer a visible personality, an all-powerful king ... the center now lies in the system itself, invisible but omnipresent'.[40] By this account, society itself becomes a representational device – one huge automatism or mechanism. An 'invisible' raster of relationships displaces the human 'king' or animator.

Can the operation of this silent, indeterminate 'system' be revealed? One would need a diagnostic test pattern designed to animate and render sensible the material and mechanical 'noise' of cultural representations, their nodal points of interference and failure. Modern art serves this redeeming social function: it tests the mechanistic mediums that provide our information and channels of communication, probing whatever seems automatic, that is to say, natural to the medium. The test often takes the form of a hand-rendering of the imagery produced by mechanical and electronic technologies. It is not a matter of giving the new medium a soul, for it has one already. The problem is to locate where the soul lies – now – at the present, unique historical moment.

40 Lewis Mumford, 'Authoritarian and Democratic Technics', *Technology and Culture*, 5, Winter 1964, p.5.

The 'pensive spectator' revisited:
time and its passing in the still and moving image.
Laura Mulvey

I am arguing that the cinema in the age of the digital will remain the same. Yes, it will remain the same and it will be utterly different. For...the digital is not only a new technique of post-production work or a new delivery system or storage medium, it is the new horizon for thinking about cinema, which also means that it gives a vantage point beyond the horizon, so that we can, as it were, try to look back to where we actually are, and how we arrived there. The digital can thus function as a time machine, a conceptual boundary as well as its threshold.[1]

My opening proposition – that electronic and digital technologies have recently had a significant impact on celluloid based cinema – is obvious, even to the point of banality. My hope here is, first of all, to bring out some of the implications for film criticism and film history that might lie behind the obviousness, most particularly how technological change has given a new kind of visibility to stillness as a property of celluloid. I say 'celluloid' advisedly as my interest, in the first instance, lies in the interaction between the old, mechanical technology (associated with cinema) and the new, electronic or digital technologies. That is, how a cinema that was not conscious of the implications of future technology might be affected, even enhanced, by refraction through the new. I have been trying to imagine a dialectical relationship here, where the old and the new react with each other to create innovative ways of thinking about the language of cinema and its significance at the present historical moment.

I started writing about the cinema and thinking about it theoretically in the early 1970s, so juxtaposition between 'old' and 'new' must also refer to my own attitudes and approaches. Using new technology as, in Thomas Elsaesser's term, 'a new horizon' to look back at the cinema of the past has pushed me also to return to, and attempt to reconfigure, the main theoretical lines of approach that have influenced my thought. This process has been like an experiment, trying out, in changed conditions, the theories that I have been applying to film for so long. There are three points of departure. First of all, spectatorship: radical changes in the material, physical, ways in which the cinema is consumed necessarily demand that theories of spectatorship should be reconfigured. Secondly; the indexical sign: the fact that the digital can mimic analogue images, as well as doctoring them, gives a new significance

1 Thomas Elsaesser: 'Digital Cinema: Delivery, Time, Event' in T. Elsaesser and K.Hoffmann (eds) *Cinema Futures: Cain, Abel or Cable? The Screen Arts in the Digital Age.* Amsterdam University Press, Amsterdam 1998 pp. 204-5.

2 Annette Michelson has
described the 'heady delights
of the editing table': 'the sense
of control, of repetition,
acceleration, deceleration,
arrest in freeze-frame, release,
and reversal of movement is
inseparable from the thrill
of power.'

to the direct registration of the pro-filmic on celluloid. And finally, narrative: analysis of cinematic narrative that assumes an essentially linearity, a dependence on cause and effect and on closure, shifts with non-linear viewing. All these inflections are derived, above all, from the viewer's new command over viewing technology and, most of all, the freedom given by the technology over the pace and order of a film. As narrative coherence fragments, as the index suddenly finds visibility in the slowed or stilled image, so spectatorship finds new forms. Out of the paradox or contradiction based on technology, a dialectical relation, with implications for aesthetics and concepts, might begin to emerge.

When I first started writing about cinema in the early 1970s' films had always been seen in darkened rooms, projected at twenty four (or thereabouts) frames a second. Only professionals, directors and editors, had easy access to the flat bed editing tables that broke down the speed needed to create the illusion of 'natural' movement.[2] Then, I was pre-occupied by Hollywood's ability to construct the female star as ultimate spectacle, the emblem and guarantee of its fascination and power. Now, I am more interested in the way that those moments of spectacle were also moments of narrative halt, a state of near stillness, that figure the halt and the stillness inherent in the structure of celluloid itself. Then, I was concerned with the way Hollywood eroticised the pleasure of looking, inscribing a sanitised voyeurism into its style and narrative conventions. Now, I am more interested in the ways in which the presence of time itself can be discovered behind the mask of storytelling.

The paradox: new technologies (might) reveal aspects of the cinema's beauty or interest, they do this across media, in the passage from celluloid to the electronic. This displacement breaks the bond of specificity that was so important to my generation of filmmakers and theorists as both a theoretical and aesthetic principle. But, on the other hand, as new technologies open up, for instance, access to the cinema's own paradoxical relation between movement and stillness, this in turn allows the spectator time to stop and look and think. Anyone can use electronic media's inter-activity, stop the flow of film and find a fascination in the still image that had previously been concealed by movement. This process then can open up a space in which the aesthetics of celluloid meet those of the photograph; the kind of theoretical reflection developed within an analysis of the still photograph finds a new relevance for the moving image. To start with, I want to try to approach the theoretical implications of these issues through a short summary of some aspects of the fraught but also productive relationship between still and moving images in the cinema.

The problem: does the temporal property of the index, its link to a moment in time, a quality so easily and consciously attributed to the still photograph, tend to get lost in the moving image? And then: if stillness does appear in the moving image, does the index find visibility? These questions involve a return to familiar ground for photographic theory and to some of the most well known sites of its discussion and elaboration. But these reflections might, now, have new relevance for cinematic theory.

Roland Barthes, unsurprisingly, provides a point of departure. *Camera Lucida* establishes key attributes of the still photograph's relation to time. Most particularly, Barthes suggests that as the photographic image embalms a moment of time it also embalms an image of life halted, which eventually – with the actual passing of time – will become an image of life after death. In numerous passages, he associates the photographic image with death. But he denies that this touching presence of embalmed time and life halted can appear in cinema. Not only does the cinema have no 'punctum' but it also both loses and disguises its relation to the temporality that is characteristic of the still photograph. In the first instance, this is due to movement:

> *In the cinema, whose raw material is photographic, the image does not, however, have this completeness (which is fortunate for the cinema). Why? Because the photograph, taken in flux, is impelled, ceaselessly drawn towards other views; in the cinema, no doubt, there is always a photographic referent, but this referent shifts, it does not make a claim in favour of its reality, it does not protest its former existence; it does not cling to me: it is not a* specter.[3]

Furthermore:

> *The cinema participates in the domestication of Photography – at least the fictional cinema, precisely the one said to be the seventh art; a film can be mad by artifice, can present signs of cultural madness, it is never mad by nature (by iconic status); it is the very opposite of a hallucination; it is simply an illusion; its vision is oneiric, not ecmnesic.*[4]

Barthes draws attention to two major considerations here. First of all there is movement: the movement essential for cinematographic technology to function as the celluloid travels through the machine, further enhanced by the camera's own ability to move. Secondly there is fiction: the conceptual and ideological properties of storytelling. Between the two exists the 'objective alliance' that links cinema's mechanical forward movement, the illusion of movement and the movement of narrative. This prioritisation of movement has dominated cinema from its origins (although avant-garde movements have continually rebelled against it), and now is beginning to blur as celluloid is displaced onto technologies that allow access to an illusion of its inherent stillness. In the new technological era, with different hierarchies and changing priorities, movement is just one property among others.

3 Roland Barthes: *Camera Lucida*. Vintage, London 1993 p. 89.

4 Ibid. p.117.

Raymond Bellour paraphrases Barthes' distinction between the photograph and the cinema saying:

On one side there is movement, the present, presence; on the other, immobility, the past, a certain absence. On one side, the consent of illusion; on the other a quest for hallucination. Here a fleeting image, one that seizes us in flight; there a completely still image that cannot be fully grasped. On this side, time doubles life; on that time returns to us brushed by death.[5]

5 Raymond Bellour: 'The Pensive Spectator' *Wide Angle* Vol.9 No.1 p.6. Christian Metz also points out that the immobility and silence of the still photograph, with its connotation of death, disappears in the moving image. See Christian Metz, 'Photography and Fetish', *October*, no.34, Fall 1985, pp.81-90.

The question of cinema's relation to fiction is central here and leads directly to the film fiction's 'double temporality'. Unlike written or oral narratives a fundamental duality of conflicting temporalities lie at the heart of narrative cinema. Firstly, there is the moment of registration; the moment when the image in front of the lens is inscribed by light onto photosensitive material passing behind the lens. Each frame is exposed singly, as though it were a still photograph. This process of inscription, the physical link between the object and its image, is, in semiotic terms, an index. The index is the source of the image's place in time, its relation to the past that gives it, in common with the still photograph, its characteristic 'there-and-then-ness'. However, this primary presence of time suspended needs to be absorbed into and masked by the time of the story time which enables fiction's diegetic world to assert its validity and for the cinema to spin the magic that makes its story-telling work. Just as the still frame is absorbed into the illusion of movement of narrative, so does the 'then-ness', the presence of the moment of registration associated with the aesthetics of still photography, have to lose itself in the temporality of the narrative and its fictional world. There is a presence, a 'here-and-now-ness', that the cinema asserts through its 'objective alliance' with story-telling. Such an assertion of a fictional present down plays, even represses, the aesthetic attributes cinema shares with the photograph.

To summarise: cinematic narrative asserts its own temporality. Everyone knows that the moving image has difficulties with tense; thus the use of clumsy flashbacks, calendar leaves flipping forward, etc. On the other hand, its temporal ambiguities may be exploited for aesthetic purposes, as, for instance, in *Last Year at Marienbad*. But all these devices, whether clumsy or complicated, tend to remain within the temporality demanded by the story and the 'there-ness' and the 'then-ness' of the film's original moment, its moment of registration, stays hidden.

However, Bellour goes on to point out that, at certain moments within a fiction, the film's original, repressed time can break through and find a momentary presence. Even if the spectator is unable to halt time in the cinema, films can, and indeed often do, refer to stillness by direct reference to photography within a given story.

*What happens when the spectator of a film is confronted with a photograph?
The photo becomes first one object among many; like all other elements of a film,
the photograph is caught up in the film's unfolding. Yet the presence of a photo
on the screen gives rise to very particular trouble. Without ceasing to advance its
own rhythm, the film seems to freeze, to suspend itself, inspiring in the spectator
a recoil from the image that goes hand in hand with a growing fascination...
Creating another distance, another time, the photo permits me to reflect on
the cinema.* [6]

And he then ends with:

*As soon as you stop the film, you begin to find time to add to the image. You
start to reflect differently on film, on cinema. You are led towards the photogram
– which is itself a step further in the direction of the photograph. In the frozen
film (or photogram), the presence of the photograph bursts forth, while other
means exploited by the mise-en-scene to work against time tend to vanish. The
photo thus becomes a stop within a stop, a freeze frame within a freeze frame;
between it and the film from which it emerges, two kinds of time blend together,
always inextricable but without becoming confused. In this the photograph
enjoys a privilege over all other effects that make the spectator, this hurried
spectator, a pensive one as well.* [7]

Here, Bellour makes a crucially important connection between the halting
of narrative, the eruption of the still within the film, and a shift in the nature
of spectatorship that also affects the representation of time. The appearance
of a still image gives a greater degree of visibility to the moment of registration
and, out of that space in narrative flow, the 'pensive' spectator is enabled to
reflect upon and experience the kind of reverie that Barthes had associated
only with the photograph.

The time of registration and the time of the fiction are in tension with
each other and have often been taken to stand in polar opposition, marking
the difference between illusion and materiality. At this point, there might well
seem to be a hidden agenda emerging from behind my argument. To strip
away narrative and reveal the actualities of both celluloid and the cinematic
apparatus resonates with the materialist, avant-gardist aspiration of the 1960s
and 1970s. There is definitely, of course, an element of this in my argument.
On the other hand, the cinematic representation of time cannot be exactly
pinned down or stabilised; it contains its own dialectic between stillness and
movement that goes beyond the opposition between the illusion and the
material. This has always been an aesthetic advantage for cinema and has
been exploited by the most interesting directors and filmmakers across the
spectrum from classical cinema to avant-garde film. For instance, Raymond
Bellour's example of stillness is taken from Max Ophuls' *Letter from an*

6 Bellour, op.cit. pp. 6-7.

7 Ibid. p.10

Unknown Woman, whilst Hollis Frampton's (*nostalgia*) bears witness to a fascination with temporal paradox and contradiction. But there are two further considerations here. First of all, the translation from one medium to another introduces a relationship between old and new and thus a further dimension of temporality that is, in itself, elusive. Secondly, the sensation of 'then-ness' associated with the photographic index is mixed with uncertainty and remains outside any easy designation. Both uncertainties lead to the difficulty of conceptualising time and its close connection to human mortality.

In *Camera Lucida*, Barthes tries to pin down this elusive relation to time. For him, the photograph's fascination lies in its continued assertion of its indexical moment: a 'then' that persists into 'now'. He resorts to using 'shifters', those parts of speech that can vary according to the speaker's position in time and/ or space, thereby evoking this disturbing, *trompe l'oeil*, effect. 'Was' and 'is' and 'this' and 'that' join 'then' and 'now'. The temporal complexity of the index persists into the cinema, potentially creating a strong pull towards the reality of registration as a moment of stillness or seizure. On the other hand, cinema is a medium of duration. A film unfolds; its movement through time has to have an initial starting point that refers to a future closing point. And this momentum is often further overlaid by the temporalities of fiction.

The passing of time itself affects what is seen on the screen. So much of cinema history now belongs to historical time and the people depicted on the screen as living, animate beings, from insignificant passer-by to major Hollywood stars, are now dead. Temporalities begin to blur and the intractable, indexical, pastness of the cinematic image begins to make itself more visible to consciousness and imagination. Siegfried Kracauer, writing in the 1950s, reflects on the way old films depicting the settings and milieux of one's earlier life, at first seem absurd and then suddenly change their meaning:

> *As he laughs at them, however, he is bound to realise, shudderingly that he has been spirited away into the lumber-room of his private self... In a flash the camera exposes the paraphernalia of our former existence, stripping them of the significance that originally transfigured them so they are changed from things in their own right into invisible conduits.'* [8]

He describes this sense of being revisited by the past as it is channelled through film into the present, precipitating the kind of involuntary memory that itself confuses time:

> *The thrill of these old films is that they bring us face to face with the inchoate, cocoon-like world from which we come – all the objects, or rather the sediments of objects, that were our companions in a pupa state ... Numerous films ...draw on the incomparable spell of those near and far away days which mark the border region between the present and the past. Beyond it the realm of history begins.'* [9]

8 Siegfried Kracauer: *Theory of Film*. Princeton University Press 1997 Princeton p 56.

9 Ibid. p.57.

Alongside the passing of time, new technologies give the spectator control of the viewing process. Now, by stilling or slowing movie images, the time of the film's original moment of registration suddenly bursts through its artificial, narrative, surface. The cohesion of the story begins to crumble and other elements seep into and interact with the narrative. Another moment of time, behind the fictional time of the story, begins to emerge through this kind of fragmentation and excavation of a sequence or film fragment. The film acquires a transparency, so that other levels or planes essential to the cinema can make themselves felt. The process may, perhaps, be compared to a stretching out of material on which the printed pattern begins to reveal other, hidden, textures and meanings. Even in the case of a Hollywood movie, beyond the story is the indexical imprint of the pro-filmic scene: the set, the stars, the extras take on the immediacy and presence of a document and the fascination of time fossilised can overwhelm and halt the fascination of narrative progression. The 'nowness' of story time gives way to the 'then-ness' of the movie's own moment in history. But even as this process of transformation, or, distanciation, takes place, the two kinds of time rub against and affect each other. The flow of the story can give way to the presence of document, while a shot stilled can emphasise a gesture or look that enhances and illuminates a character or event in the narrative.

As cinema ages, its aesthetic polarities critically analysed throughout its history seem to become less important in their differences and more important in their dialectical relations with each other. Rather than diverging into an either/or, for instance, specificity of the film-strip verses illusion of movement, fiction verses document, grounding in reality verses potential for fantasy, these aspects of the celluloid-based medium move closer together. Movement-image based cinema and time-image based cinema flow across each other more freely as cinema's own history lengthens, opening up conduits that complement rather than contradict Deleuze's film aesthetic. Passing time, in itself, shifts perception of relations and aesthetic patterns and these shifts are, in turn, accentuated by the new horizons formed by new technologies. As a result perhaps a new kind of ontology may emerge, in which ambivalence, impurity and uncertainty displace the traditional oppositions. Cinema's inherent, but often divergent, possibilities not only seem in retrospect more compatible but also to have had more complex relations, more dialectical interaction. In this possible aesthetic, interest lies in cinema's potential for shifting its form and for mutating its being, creating the trompe l'oeil effect in which uncertainty is, at the same time, a certainty because its magic works without recourse to deception or dissimulation. From this perspective, cinema becomes more, rather than less, complicated and moments or movies that bring out this potential for ambivalence become correspondingly more significant.

* * *

The different possibilities of film consumption brought about by new technologies have transformed both an understanding of spectatorship – my own longstanding theoretical point of engagement with cinema – and also forms of textual analysis as a key method of critical practice.[10] The concept of the voyeuristic spectator, which I developed in my earlier writings, depended, in the first instance, upon certain material conditions of cinema exhibition: the darkness of the auditorium, the projector beam lighting up the screen, the procession of images that imposed their own rhythm on the spectator's attention. And, of course, it was the particular structure of this kind of spectacle that the Hollywood studios refined so perfectly. In counter distinction, I later tried to evolve an alternative spectator who was driven by curiosity and by the desire to decipher the screen. The curious spectator was, perhaps, an intellectual, informed by feminism and the avant-garde. The idea of curiosity as a drive to see, but also to know, still marked a utopian space in which the cinema might respond to the human mind's longstanding interest in puzzles and riddles. This spectator may be the ancestor of the one now formed by those new modes of consumption that open up the pleasures of the hidden cinema to anyone who cares to experiment with the equipment available.

I have, in the first instance, attempted to adapt Raymond Bellour's concept of the pensive spectator in order to evoke the thoughtful reflection on the film image that is now possible, a way of seeing into the screen's images, stretching them into new dimensions of time and space. The pleasure in the fragment leads to the pleasure in the still itself. Here the pensive spectator can confront the film's original moment of registration, revealed once the narrative's ornament has been stripped away. With the hybrid relationship between the celluloid original and its new electronic carrier, there is time to reflect on time itself and on the presence of the past and on the 'then-ness' of the photographic process. It would seem that the pensive spectator might be able to rescue those aspects of the cinema that Roland Barthes felt were lacking next to the complexity of the photograph. It might be possible for cinema to 'make a claim in favour of its reality', to 'protest its former existence', and for its investment in emotional detail 'to cling to me'. Certainly, the cinema is increasingly inhabited by spectres. Similarly, the oppositions extracted by Raymond Bellour that evoke the different attributes of film and photography, are now producing new relations and connections to each other, sequentially or simultaneously,

out of which a new oscillating image of time may be beginning to emerge.
Movement gives way to immobility, the present tense of movement is interrupted
by the sudden eruption of stillness and the past, and absence becomes presence.
On the other hand, there is an even more acute sense that time cannot be
grasped and that 'time that doubles life' returns all the more clearly 'brushed
by death'.

I have argued for the pensive spectator's relation to curiosity, even to
cinephilia. But the pensive spectator may also be 'fetishistic'. The slowing
down and stilling process opens up new areas of fascination especially in
relationship to the human figure. Certain privileged moments can become
fetishised moments for endless and obsessive repetition, while a star or a
performance can suddenly acquire a further dimension of fascination once
freed from their subordination to narrative. This new, freely accessible
stillness or slowness, extracted from the moving image, is a product of the
paradoxical relation between celluloid and new technology. It is primarily the
historic cinema of celluloid that can blossom into new significance and beauty
when its original stillness, its material existence in the photogram, is revealed
in this way. The cinema has always been a medium of revelation and, once
again, there is a paradox here. The magic of cinema has been identified,
throughout its history, with its ability to simulate movement. In very early
film demonstrations, this element of revelation could be built into the staging
of the show. The projection might start with a stilled image, a projected
photograph. Suddenly, the image would come to life and the magic of cinema
would infuse the screen. Now, perhaps, the magical moment, perversely and
paradoxically, comes with a reversal of direction: a new fascination comes
into being when the moving image is stilled. The new, from this perspective,
allows a fresh and unfamiliar insight into the old. Just as the early theorists
of film celebrated the way that the camera could reveal more of the world than
was perceptible to the naked eye, now the pensive spectator can discover more
in the celluloid image than could be seen at twenty four frames per second.

My reworking of Raymond Bellour's concept of the pensive spectator
depends on the paradox that I introduced towards the beginning of this essay:
that our capacity to look into the cinema's celluloid images is a product of new
technologies. This, of course, brings yet another element into this picture of
displacements, hybrids and reverberations. Thomas Elsaesser's vision of the
digital as a 'horizon' for thinking about the nature of the cinema is coupled
with the digital as 'time machine'. Both suggest a knight's move beyond the
confines of the media themselves, in which time itself becomes a subject for
thought, but also for reverie and for the imagination: how time is inscribed

into culture, and how it becomes lost in the elusiveness of history. Of course, this is really only a metaphor – but one that can perhaps be activated by the presence of time halted.

Safety in Numbness:
Some remarks on problems of 'Late Photography'
David Campany

Several weeks into the intensive coverage of the aftermath of the collapse of
the World Trade Centre, Britain's Channel Four News screened a thirty-minute
special report entitled *Reflections on Ground Zero*. It followed New York photographer Joel Meyerowitz as he manoeuvred diligently around the smoking
rubble and cranes with his large format camera. He had been commissioned
by the Museum of the City of New York to make for posterity the 'official'
images of the scene and the clean-up operation. He was granted exclusive
photographic access to the site and produced a substantial body of colour
photographs, exhibited in the city and later internationally. (Figures 19 & 20)
Just about everyone worldwide with access to a television had seen the strike
on the towers. The ensuing news reports were transmitted globally, electronically
and instantaneously. Lower Manhattan became the most imaged and visible
of places, the epicentre of a vast amount of state of the art news production.
Nevertheless here was a report featuring a solitary man, his tripod and his
forty-five pound, sixty-year old Deardorff camera. It was a slow and deliberating
half-hour, imbued throughout with a sense of melancholy by the constant
tinkling of a piano in a minor key. There was an air of ritual too, since this
was at least part of the function of both the programme and the photographs.
Yet the most telling aspect of the feature was the contrast drawn between the
complexity of the geopolitical situation and the simplicity of Meyerowitz'
camera and working method. There was a suggestion that photography,
rather than television might be the better medium for official history. The
photographs were being positioned as superior to the programme in which
they were presented.

The programme contained video images at least as informative and
descriptive as the photographs, yet television was presenting itself as unable
to perform a task given over to photography. Meyerowitz was filmed telling us
at one point: 'I felt if there was no photographic record allowed, then it was
history erased'.[1] No doubt this special status will symbolically structure how
his pictures are seen as they tour. Even so this will probably become less

1 To further extend and deepen
the tension between photography and other technologies
that incorporate it, let me say
right away that I have had my
closest look at Meyerowitz'
images via the internet, having
seen them firstly on television
and secondly in exhibition
*After September 11: Images
From Ground Zero* held at
The Museum of London.
The exhibition was organised
by the Bureau of Educational
and Cultural Affairs of the U.S.
Department of State in
conjunction with the Museum
of the City of New York.

2 Meyerowitz says at another point in the programme, 'I had to do this so that people in future generations could look at this site and see the wound that was received here, the aftermath of the blow, and to see what it took to repair it, what it looked like everywhere in this sixteen acre site. Somebody had to have the consciousness to do it'

3 Peter Wollen, 'Vectors of Melancholy', in Ralph Rugoff, ed., *The Scene of the Crime*, MIT Press, Cambridge, Mass. and London, 1997. See also Thierry de Duve's essay 'Time Exposure and Snapshot: The Photograph as Paradox', *October*, no. 5, 1978, which makes a similar opposition.

4 See, in particular, Roland Barthes, *Camera Lucida. Reflections on Photography*, Farrar, Strauss, Giroux, New York, 1980 and Walter Benjamin, 'The Work of Art in the Age of Mechanical Reproduction' (1936) in his *Illuminations*, Jonathan Cape, London, 1970. For broader discussions of the subject see Celia Lury, *Prosthetic Culture: photography, memory, identity*, Routledge, London, 1997; Scott McQuire, Visions of Modernity, Sage, London, 1998) and Eduardo Cadava, *Words of Light: Theses on the Photography of History*, Princeton University Press, New Jersey, 1997.

secure in the future – it is likely that they will take up a place alongside so many other images in the constructions of history. What *may* mark them out in posterity is the very act of sanctioning itself, the idea that there was a need, a desire, to nominate an official body of images, and that these should be photographs.[2]

Meyerowitz' imagery is not so much the trace of an event as the *trace of the trace of an event*. His 'late' photography is a particularly clear instance of an approach that is becoming a commonplace use of the medium. What are we to make of the highly visible turn toward photographing the aftermath of events – traces, fragments, empty buildings, empty streets, damage to the body and damage to the world? These images appear to us as particularly static, often sombre and quite 'straight' kinds of pictures. They assume an aesthetic of utility closer to forensic photography than traditional photojournalism. They are, what Peter Wollen recently called, 'cool photography' as opposed to the dramatic 'hot' photography of events.[3] Sometimes we can see that something has happened, sometimes we are left to imagine or project it, or to be informed about it by other means. The images often contain no people, but a lot of remnants of activity. If this type of image was only present in contemporary art it might be overlooked as a passing trend (of all art's media photography is still the most subject to curatorial whim). But we see it increasingly in new photojournalism, documentary, campaign work and even news, advertising and fashion. One might easily surmise that photography has of late inherited a major role as an undertaker, summariser or accountant. It turns up late, wanders through the places where things have happened totting up the effects of the world's activity. This is a kind of photograph that foregoes the representation of events in progress and so cedes them to other media. As a result it is quite different from the spontaneous snapshot and has a different relation to memory and to history.

The theoretical framework connecting the photograph to collective memory is as well established as it is complex. The photograph can be an aid to memory, but it can also become an obstacle that blocks access to the understanding of the past. It can paralyse the personal and political ability to think beyond the image in the always fraught project of remembrance.[4] However, in the popular culture of mass media, the frozen image is often used as a simple signifier of the memorable, as if there were a straightforward connection between the functions of memory and the 'freezing' capabilities of the still camera. Indeed this is such a well-established assumption about photographs that to even question it seems a little perverse. So rather than thinking about a direct relation between the photograph and memory let us think about the two of them in relation to other media.

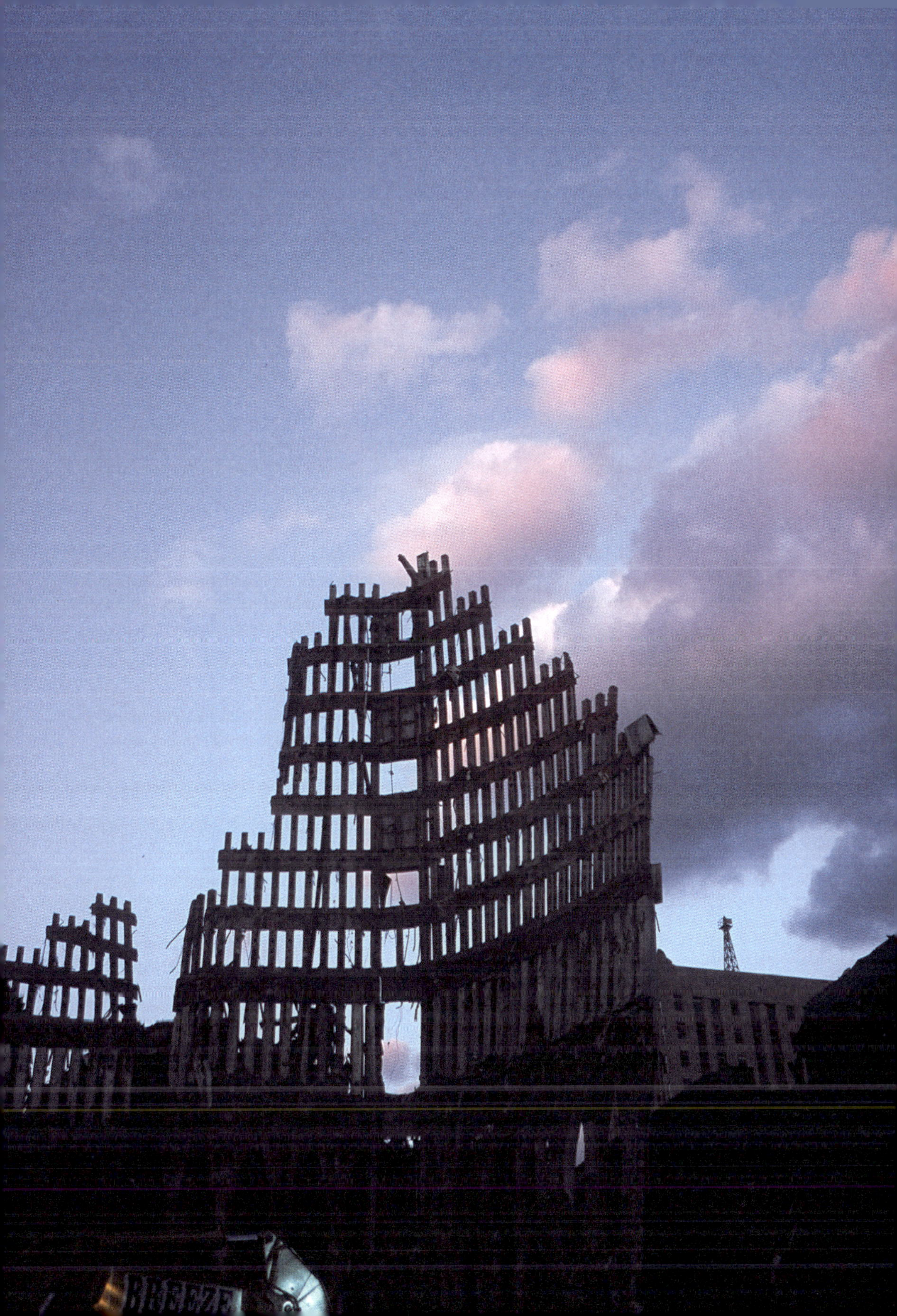
BREEZE

Television and cinema make regular use of photographic snapshots and freeze-frames as a kind of instant history or memory that they, as moving images, are not. Indeed it seems plausible that it is this kind of use of the still photograph that has cemented the popular connection of photography with memory, rather than their being some intrinsic relationship. There is nothing like the 'presentness' of the moving image to emphasise the 'pastness' of the photograph. It does this even more effectively than the continuum of life itself because as a technology the still image is a part or a ghost of the moving image. It is its memory or primitive ancestor. Yet to presume that the still image or the freeze-frame is inherently more memorable or closer to the nature of memory, is to overlook the fact that the very operation of our memory is changing. It is shaped by the image world around us. The structure of memory is, in large measure, culturally determined by the means of representation at our disposal. As our image world shifts in character, so do our conditions of remembrance.[5] It may well be that the special status granted the still photograph in the era of television and newer technologies is not so much a recognition of its mnemonic superiority, as a nostalgic wish that it still might have such 'power'. This is to say there is an investment in the idea that the relative primitivism of photography will somehow rescue the processes of our memory that have been made so complicated by the sheer amount of information we assimilate from diverse of technologies.

In popular consciousness (as opposed to popular *unconsciousness*) the still image continues to be thought of as being more memorable than those that move. Yet if the frozen photograph seems memorable in the contemporary media-sphere it is probably because it *says* very little. It relies for support upon the surfeit of audio-visual information in the culture at large. Its very muteness allows it to appear somehow uncontaminated by the noise of the televisual.[6] While its privileged status may be imagined to stem from a natural capacity to condense and simplify things, the effects of the still image derive much more from its capacity to remain radically open, radically laconic. It is not that a photograph naturally says a thousand words, rather that a thousand words can be said about it. This is why television and film tend to use the still image only for contrived and highly rhetorical moments of pathos, tension and melancholy.

That said, the static photograph taken after an event, rather than the frozen image made of it, is the radically open image par excellence. It is 'pre-frozen', the stillness of the image complementing the stillness of the aftermath. So, of course, it isn't the kind of photograph used ordinarily by television and film to evoke the memorable. Indeed television is usually very wary of this kind of image as it confuses the character of stillness ('Is this a photograph or is this a continuous shot of an immobile scene?') When it is

5 See Laura Mulvey's discussion of the reconfiguration of memory by the new technologies of spectatorship elsewhere in this volume.

6 An unnamed New Yorker in the television programme I am discussing declares at one point, 'People wili come back to Joel's [Meyerowitz'] photographs. They have a very powerful silence in them. They are very still'.

used, as in the case of the programme on Meyerowitz' project, the stillness is emphasised and defined for the viewer by a restless use of the rostrum camera zooming into details and roaming about the photographic frame.

To think through the current turn toward the 'late photograph' it is instructive to think about images taken before, during and after events. I mean this in two senses. The first is the usual one – literally, photographs taken before, during and after a particular occurrence. However we could also think more broadly of three phases of the social history of photography. Over its one hundred and sixty year history, there was a finite period in which photography carried the weight of events and defined what an event was. For several decades the medium was slow and cumbersome both in its technical procedures and in its means of social distribution. Only from the 1920s, with the rapid expansion of the mass media, the growing dominance of print journalism, and technical developments within photographic technology itself, did photography become the definitive medium and modulator of the event as a moment, an instant, something that could be frozen and examined. Good photo-reporters were thought to be those who followed the action. The goal was to be in the right place at the right time 'as things happened'. This lasted until the late 1960s and early 1970s with the standardised introduction into journalism of portable video cameras. Over the last few decades, it has become clear that the conception of events was supplanted by video and then dispersed in recent years across a variety of media technologies. In this situation, photographers often prefer to wait until the noise has died down and the event is over. The still cameras are loaded as the video cameras are packed away. The photographs taken come not just in the aftermath of the event but also in the aftermath of video. What we see first 'live' or at least in real time on television might be revisited by a photography that depicts stillness rather than freezing things. Photojournalists used to be at the centre of the event because photography was at the centre of culture. Today they are as likely to be at the scene of the aftermath because photography is, in relative terms, at the aftermath of culture. Photography is much less the means by which the event is grasped. We have learned to expect more from a situation than a frozen image (even though in the climate of emotive news television we might be offered the static image as an ideological 'distillation', a mythic summary). Video gives us things as they happen. They may be manipulated, they may be misrepresented and undigested but they happen in the present tense. Today it is very rare that photographs actually break the news. The newspaper constitutes only a second wave of interpreted information or commentary. Furthermore when 'late photographs' appear in the slower forms of the illustrated magazine or gallery exhibit they are at one further remove.[7]

7 It might be argued, however, that in such circumstances it becomes possible to look at the overlooked or unreported.

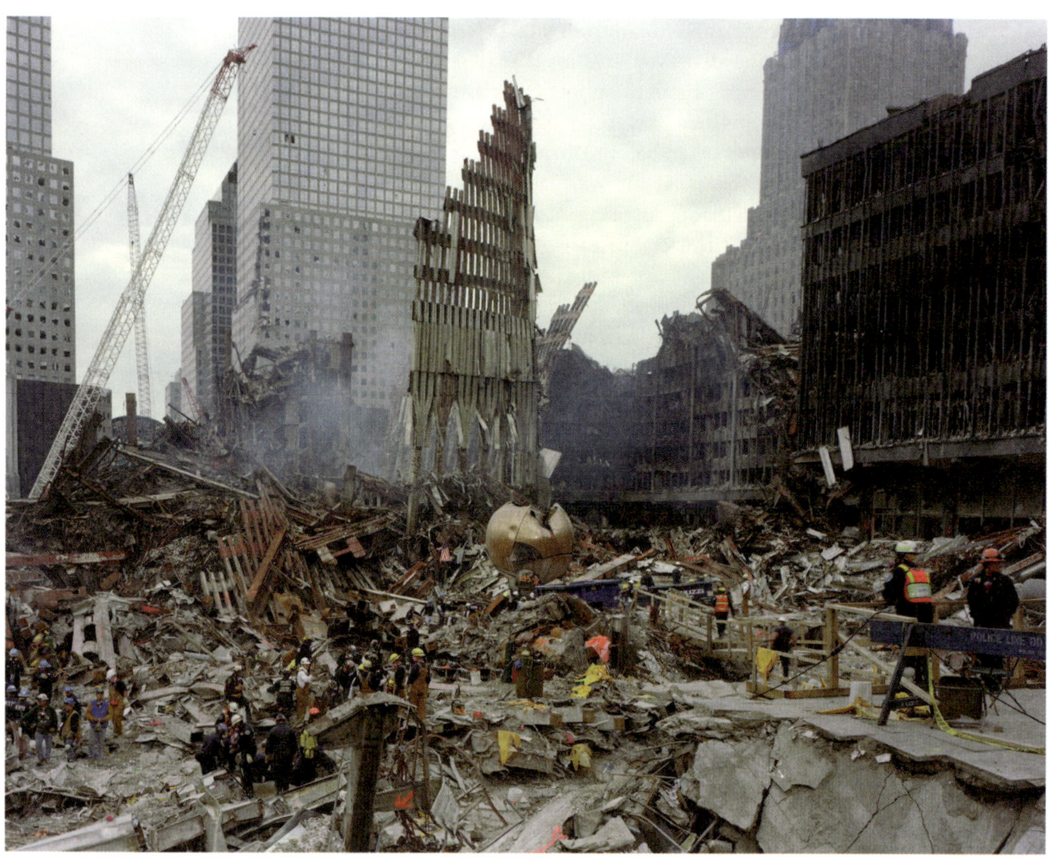

Figure 20. Joel Meyerowitz, *Rescue Teams on the Plaza, September 27, 2001*

Late twentieth and twenty-first century photography takes on something of the visual character of those celebrated nineteenth century images of battlefields such as Roger Fenton's photography of the exhausted terrains of the Crimea from the 1850s, or Matthew Brady's images of the scarred earth and corpses of the American Civil War from the following decade. Yet this is a false homology in key respects. The similarity masks the radical changes that have taken place in our image culture since then. Consider, for example, the question of stillness. Although it might be a scientific truism that photographs are still, this fact is always subject to cultural and historical interpretation. Those nineteenth century photographs were not still in the way in which we think of stillness today. I don't mean this in the sense that things moved during long exposures (which we all know they did). They weren't still because nearly all images of that time were still. That is to say, the immobility of the photograph would be almost too obvious to mention. Stillness in photographs only became apparent and definitive in the presence of the moving image. The whole drive toward precision, the stopping of time and freezing of action takes place in the era of cinema. Cinema, we could say, was not just the invention of the moving image, it was also the invention of the stillness of photography. In the era of cinema, the frozenness of the snapshot – professionalised in photojournalism, democratised in amateurism – came to be understood as the essence of the photographic. It found its exemplary instance in the middle of the twentieth century with the notion of the 'decisive moment' where the speedy modernity of the now cinematized world is arrested by the speedy modernity of the handheld, high speed and compact still camera.

However in the era of video, photography loses this monopoly on stillness and immediacy. This is a material circumstance and a social one: as a technology the video image is stoppable, repeatable, cheap and quick; and institutionally it has come to be used in many of the roles formerly held by photography. It is interesting that a recent book on the history of photojournalism opts to conclude in the mid-1970s, in an attempt to contrive a clean and dignified end.[8] To be sure, the influence of photojournalism has declined since then. Images from its heyday now find a questionable afterlife in the coffee table book, while many of its vestigial forms have turned into pastiches of a glorious past for colour supplements and audiences who prefer an air of aesthetic classicism. Yet announcements of the 'death of photojournalism' are quite premature. If it faced its demise in the 1970s it was only insofar as it was mistakenly assumed that its only possible significance could derive from a monopoly over stillness and over our comprehension of events. The last couple of decades have seen a coming to terms with photography's historical situation on the part of many photographers and writers. Redefinitions of the possibilities of photojournalism are beginning to emerge which seek out new contexts and they touch on the kinds of approach I am discussing here. But first let me to sketch in a little more of photojournalism's past.

If the war in Vietnam is regarded as the last 'photographer's war', this is as much a function of the shifting nature of warfare as it is of media coverage. Vietnam was chaotic on two levels. The environment was messy (and mess is highly photogenic), and U.S. military and political policy was erratic. As a result the conflict was prolonged, increasing the photographer's picture making opportunities. By contrast the Gulf War is often described as the first war experienced in terms of image simulation. What few images we saw were satellite images from news journalists along with abstracted military footage

8 Robert Lebeck and Bodo von Dewitz, eds., Kiosk: A History of Photojournalism, Steidl, Gottingen, Germany, 2002.

9 For an account of those press photographs that were made during the Gulf War see John Taylor's 'The Gulf War in the Press', *Portfolio Magazine*, no. 11, Summer 1991. For an account of virtual representation see Jean Baudrillard, *The Gulf War Did Not Take Place*, Power Publications, 1995, and Tim Druckrey, 'Deadly Representations or Apocalypse Now', *Ten/8*, vol. 2, no. 2, 1991.

10 For a useful discussion of this see Stanley Cavell, *The World Viewed*, (enlarged edition), Harvard University Press, 1979.

11 Interestingly, Meyerowitz is a photographer who first came to prominence shooting 'decisive moments' on the streets of New York, deeply influenced by Henri Cartier-Bresson. As his career moved on there was a general shift from those fleeting snapshots to a slower way of working with a large camera, and from a photography of 'events' to a photography of longer duration.

12 For a particularly rich discussion of allegory in recent documentary work see Justin Carville's 'Re-negotiated territory: the politics of place, space and landscape in Irish photography', *Afterimage*, vol. 29 no. 1, July/August 2001.

13 Sophie Ristelhueber, *Aftermath*, Thames & Hudson, London, 1992. The original French title was *Fait*. The artist had made a similar book in the previous decade entitled *Beirut*, Thames & Hudson, London, 1984.

and interpretive television graphics. Very few photographers covered the war.[9] They weren't allowed in. *After* the war many photographers went to Kuwait to document the leftovers – destroyed tanks, bodies, scarred desert and burning oil fields. Their images often had a post-traumatic disposition, and a mournful paralysis. And they were often accompanied by similarly melancholic writing. Photojournalism became elegiac, poetic and muted. It communicated the feeling of being outside the time of history, of events and of politics. We may have been able to see the damage afterwards, but at the cost of a sense of removal. Photography was struggling to find a way to reconcile itself with a new position beyond the event. And it was discovering that sombre melancholia was a seductive mode for the still image.

Today almost a third of all news 'photographs' are frame grabs from video and digital sources. The proportion increases in the coverage of international conflict. This has two related consequences. Firstly, there is a partial blurring of the distinction between different image technologies (resulting in a radical shift in the understanding of what photography is, what it is good at and what it is for). Secondly photography is finding other roles or, more accurately, visual culture at large is leaving photography with certain tasks and subject matters such as the aftermath. Far from being its ultimate incarnation, the decisive moment that epitomised the photographic ideal can be grasped as a historically specific ideal. The definition of a medium, particularly photo-graphy, is not autonomous or self-governing, but heteronymous, dependent on other media. It derives less from what it is *technologically* than what it is *culturally*. Photography is what we do with it. And what we do with it depends on what we do with other image technologies.[10] In the age of instantaneous and global moving images, Meyerowitz' 1942 plate camera is given a new role.[11]

It seems clear that contemporary art has a predilection for the 'late photograph'. It has become a central trope in its current dialogue with documentary. The works of Willie Doherty, Paul Seawright, Sophie Ristelhueber and Richard Misrach are some of the more interesting examples (but as I write it is hard to avoid the cheaper moodiness of images of derelict buildings and urban wastelands on display in London's galleries). There is a reticent muteness in these images that leaves them open to interpretation. Moreover their status as traces of traces fulfils for art a certain modernist reflection on the indexicality of the medium. They can also offer an allegorical, distanced reflection on the photograph as evidence and on the claims of mainstream documentary photography.[12] Tellingly the best known images made of Kuwait after the Gulf War were made by the artist Sophie Ristelhueber in her series *Fait* exhibited in galleries and museums, and published book form.[13]

In forfeiting any immediate relation to the event and taking up a slower relation to time, 'late' photographs appear to separate themselves out from the constant visual bit stream emitted by the convergence of modern electronic image technologies. Part of the appeal of these static, slow and detailed photographs is that they strike us now as being somehow a new kind of 'pure' photography that can't be confused with other kinds of image (this is no doubt another reason for their profile in museums and galleries). They look like a very *photographic* kind of photography and seem to do something no other medium does, (although as I have said, what strikes us as particularly photographic is very much subject to change). At the same time they refuse to be overtly 'creative', deploying the straight image with a mood of deliberation and detachment that chimes with a general preference in contemporary art for the slow, withdrawn and anonymous. It is telling that in the television programme *Reflections on Ground Zero* Meyerowitz opts to describe his photography as an automatic process in which creativity is avoidable: 'I was just going to be there as a witness and photograph it for what it was, without trying to put on it some formal idea of how to photograph it. I was told how to photograph it by the thing itself'. Avoiding overt 'originality' in such circumstances is an admirable aim, but we would do well to bear in mind that there really is no 'degree zero' of photography, not even at Ground Zero. Meyerowitz' images are a mixture of epic scenes, portraits and details of excavation work, all illuminated by his celebrated attention to light and atmosphere. He has skills honed over several decades of making photographs. It may be second nature to him now, but he knows what makes a good photo and can't avoid the beautiful. He certainly does have a very strong formal aesthetic even though it clearly overlaps with a popular sense of what a photographic document should look like.[14]

As I have remarked the late photograph has a long history. Art and literature have had an interest in it at least as far back as the Surrealist's appropriation of the street photographs of Eugène Atget for their stoic artlessness. Looking back over this history, writer and photographer Allan Sekula warned of the political pitfalls of decontextualising a document in order to make it enigmatic or melancholic or merely beautiful:

> *Walter Benjamin recalled the remark that Eugène Atget depicted the streets of Paris as though they were scenes of crime. That remark serves to poeticise a rather deadpan, non-expressionist style, to conflate nostalgia and the affectless instrumentality of the detective. Crime here becomes a matter of the heart as well as a matter of fact. Looking back, through Benjamin to Atget, we see the loss of the past through the continual disruptions of the urban present as a form of violence against memory, resisted by the nostalgic bohemian through acts of solipsistic, passive acquisition... I cite this example merely to raise the question*

14 Looking back over Meyerowitz' career I found myself returning to a book called *Annie on Camera* from 1982. He was one of nine photographers commissioned to make images during the production of John Huston's film *Annie*, a cheesecake musical set in depression-era New York. Meyerowitz' folio includes an image of piles of concrete rubble and broken paper-thin walls lying at the foot of slanted architectural buttresses. It was refuse discarded by set builders. He made a strikingly similar image at Ground Zero. As photographers we tend to carry visual templates around with us wherever we go, however much we feel subject matter dictates the form of our images. I wonder if Meyerowitz had the form of his knowingly fake image from *Annie* in mind when he came across the same scene twenty years later in a very different situation – a situation so many likened to something cinematic. See Nancy Grubb, ed., *Annie on Camera*, Abbeville Press, New York, 1982.

15 Allan Sekula 'Dismantling Modernism, Reinventing Documentary (Notes on the Politics of Representation)', in Terry Dennett and Jo Spence, eds., *Photography/Politics: One*, Photography Workshop, London,1980.

of the affective character of documentary. Documentary has amassed mountains of evidence. And yet, in this pictorial presentation of scientific and legalistic "fact", the genre has simultaneously contributed much to spectacle, to retinal excitation, to voyeurism, to terror, envy and nostalgia, and only a little to the critical understanding of the social world ... A truly social documentary will frame the crime, the trial, the system of justice and its official myths ... Social truth is something other than a matter of convincing style.[15]

In the light of Sekula's closing remark it is worth considering why it is that the 'late photograph' has become a 'convincing style' in contemporary culture. Its retreat from the event is no guarantee of an enlightened position or a critical stance. Its formality and visual sobriety secure nothing in and of themselves. Yet it is easy to see how it is that in an image world dispersed across screens and reconfigured in pieces, a detailed, static and resolutely perspectival rectangle can *appear* to be some kind of superior image.

Certainly the late photograph is often used as a vehicle for mass mourning or working through (Meyerowitz' *Ground Zero* project was produced primarily for New Yorkers). The danger is that it can also foster an indifference and political withdrawal that masquerades as concern. Mourning by association becomes merely an aestheticized response. There is a sense in which the late photograph in all its silence, can easily flatter the ideological paralysis of those who gaze at it with a lack of social or political will to make sense of its circumstance. In its apparent finitude and muteness it can leave us in permanent limbo, obliterating even the *need* for analysis and bolstering a kind of liberal melancholy that shuns political explanation like a vampire shuns garlic.[16] If the banal matter-of-factness of the late photograph can fill us with a sense of the sublime, it is imperative that we think through why this might be. There is a fine line between the banal and the sublime, and it is political. If an experience of the contemporary sublime derives from our being in a world beyond our comprehension, then it is a politically reified as much as an aesthetically rarefied response.

16 I borrow the simile and the general critique of the passivity of liberal ideology from Slavoj Zizek's 'Self-Interview' in *The Metastases of Enjoyment. Six Essays on Woman and Causality*, Verso, London, 1994.

Contributors

Geoffrey Batchen, an Australian cultural critic, teaches the history of photography at CUNY Graduate Center in New York. His most recent book is *Each Wild Idea: Writing, Photography, History* (MIT Press, 2001). He is curating an exhibition on the theme of photography and memory for the Van Gogh Museum in Amsterdam, due to open in March 2004.

Pavel Buchler is Research Professor of Art and Design at Manchester Metropolitan University. He is an artist and the author of *Ghost Stories*, a collection of essays on photography and film (1999).

David Campany is Senior Lecturer in the History and Theory of Photography at the Surrey Institute of Art and Design. He is the author of *Art and Photography* (Phaidon Press, forthcoming 2003). Other essays include 'Conceptual Art History or, A Home for Homes of America' in *Rewriting Conceptual Art*, ed J. Bird & M. Newman (Reaktion Books, 2000) and a contributor to the catalogue *Postcards on Photography* (Cambridge Darkroom, 1998).

Steve Edwards is Research Lecturer in Art History at the Open University. He is the editor of *Art and its Histories: a Reader*. His book *Allegories of Labour: Stories from the Archives of Photography* will be published in 2003.

David Green is Senior Lecturer in the History and Theory of Contemporary Art at the University of Brighton. He is the co-editor of *History Painting Reassessed* (Manchester University Press, 2000) and has contributed essays to Camerawork, Ten/8, Oxford Art Journal, Creative Camera, Portfolio and Contemporary Visual Arts.

Joanna Lowry is Head of Research at Kent Institute of Art and Design. She is the author of essays on the work of Douglas Gordon (in *Performing the Body, Performing the Text*, 1999), Joseph Beuys and Yves Klein (in *Sculpture and Photography*, 1998) and catalogue essays including *Rineke Dijkstra* (Photographers Gallery, 1998), *Cindy Sherman* (Hasselblad Award, Gothenburg, 1999) and *Afterglow: Ori Gersht* (2002). She has also been a regular contributor to Creative Camera, Portfolio and other photographic and contemporary art journals.

Laura Mulvey is Professor of Film and Media Studies at Birkbeck College, University of London. She is the author of *Visual and Other Pleasures* (1989), *Fetishism and Curiosity* (1996), and *Citizen Kane* (1996). She has co-directed six films with Peter Wollen including *Riddles of the Sphinx* (1978) and *Frida Kahlo and Tina Modotti* (1980) and, with artist/film-maker Mark Lewis, *Disgraced Monuments* (1994). She is currently working on a new book entitled *Death 24 x a second: Stillness and the Moving Image*.

Peter Osborne is Professor of Modern European
Philosophy at Middlesex University, London, and
an editor of the journal Radical Philosophy. His books
include: *Philosophy in Cultural Theory* (Routledge,
2000), *Conceptual Art* (edited, Phaidon, 2002)
and *Philosophies of Race and Ethnicity* (co-edited,
Continuum, 2003). Recent writing on contemporary
art includes contributions to *Victor Burgin: Relocating*
(Arnolfini, 2002) and *The Art of Tracey Emin*
(Thames and Hudson, 2002).

Olivier Richon is Head of the Photography
Department at the Royal College of Art. Artist's
publications include *Allegories* (l'Aquarium
Agnostique, Valenciennes, 2000), *After DL*
(Edition Camera Austria, 1995) and *Other Than
Itself – Writing Photography* (1989). His essay on
Orientalism, 'Re-presentation, the Harem and the
Despot' is included in the *Block Reader in Visual
Culture* (1996).

Richard Shiff is Effie Marie Cain Regents Chair
in Art and Director of the Center for the Study of
Modernism at The University of Texas at Austin.
He has published a number of theoretical essays
on nineteenth- and twentieth-century painting and
photography, including "Phototropism (Figuring
the Proper)" and "Handling Shocks: On the
Representation of Experience in Walter
Benjamin's Analogies." Much of his current work
centres on artists such as Chuck Close, who
practice both photography and painting.

Figure 1. Makers unknown (American), *Portrait of a young woman with wax flower wreath*, c.1890. Albumen print and assorted materials encased in wooden frame. 87 x 82 x 19 cm. Collection of the author.

Figure 2. Makers unknown (American); photographer: P.E. Lynne (Crookston, Minnesota), *Memorial to a Young Man*, c.1910.Albumen print on card and assorted materials encased in gilt frame. 85 x 77 x 21 cm. Collection of Arif Khan, London

Figure 3. Maker unknown (German), *Portrait of a woman*, c.1890. Albumen print on card and woven human hair encased in wooden frame. Collection of House der Fotografie, Burghausen.

Figure 4. Photographer unknown, *Portrait of a Woman*, carte de visite, c.1870. Collection of the author.

Figure 5. Photographer unknown, *Portrait of a Woman*, two cartes de visite, c.1870. Collection of the author.

Figure 6. Mason and Co., London, *Portrait of a Woman*, carte de visite. Made between 1865-74. Collection of the author.

Figure 7. John Baldassari, *The Artist is Not Merely The Slavish Announcer Of A Series of Facts, Which In This Case The Camera Has Had To Accept and Mechanically Record*, 1966-68. Photoemulsion, varnish and gesso on canvas, 59 1/8 x 45 1/8 inches. Collection of Whitney Museum of American Art, New York. Purchase with funds from the Painting and Sculpture Committee and gift of an anonymous donor.

Figure 8. Ed Ruscha, 'Conoco, Saurg, Oklahoma' from *Twentysix Gasoline Stations*, 1963. Bound artist's book. Reproduced by permission of the artist and the Gagosian Gallery.

Figure 9. Robert Barry, *Inert Gas Series: Helium. On the morning of March 6, 1969, somewhere in the Mojava Desert in California, 2 cubic feet of helium were returned to the atmosphere*, 1969. Courtesy of the artist.

Figure 10. Keith Arnatt, *Trouser-Word Piece*, 1972. Photograph and text on paper, each panel 1005 x 1005mm. Courtesy of the artist. © Tate, London, 2002.

Figure 11. Jean-Marc Bustamante. From the series *Something is Missing*, 1997 - present. Courtesy of the artist.

Figure 12. Olivier Richon, *A Real Allegory (with carrot)*, 2002. C -Type print, 50 x 60 cm.

Figure13. Willem de Kooning, *Untitled,* 1966. Charcoal on paper, 10 x 8 inches. All works by Willem de Kooning ©2003 The Willem de Kooning Foundation/Artists Rights Society, New York.

Figure 14. Chuck Close, *Self-Portrait,* 1968. Acrylic on canvas, 108 x 84 inches. Collection Walker Art Center, Minneapolis Art Center Acquisition Fund, 1969. Reproduced by permission of PaceWildenstein, New York.

Figure 15. Chuck Close, *Emma,* 2000. Oil on canvas, 72 x 60 inches. Reproduced by permission of PaceWildenstein, New York.

Figure 16. Georges Seurat, *Seated Nude Boy,* c. 1883-4. Conté crayon on paper. 31.7 x 24.7 cm. Reproduced by Permission of the National Gallery of Scotland.

Figure 17. William Henry Fox Talbot, *Oak Tree in Carclew Park*, c.1841. Calotype photograph. Reproduced by permission of the National Museum of Photography, Film and Television.

Figure 18. Georges Seurat, *Preparatory sketch for the painting La Greve Du Bas-Butin, Honfleur,* 1886. Oil on canvas, 17.2 x 26.1 cm. Reproduced by permission of The Baltimore Museum of Art.

Figure 19. Joel Meyerowitz, *The North Wall, October 26, 2001.* Courtesy of Ariel Meyerowitz Gallery, New York

Figure 20. Joel Meyerowitz, *Rescue Teams on the Plaza, September 27, 2001.* Courtesy of Ariel Meyerowitz Gallery, New York